Employing the Hard-Core Unemployed

EMPLOYING
THE HARD-CORE UNEMPLOYED

Lawrence A. Johnson

AMERICAN MANAGEMENT ASSOCIATION, INC.

This Research Study has been distributed without charge to AMA members enrolled in the General Management Division.

Photographs on pages 32, 56, 80, 100, and 165 by Bob Adelman

Standard book number: 8144–3098–8
Library of Congress catalog card number: 78–93019

About This Report

LAST FALL I VISITED North American Rockwell's NARTRANS Division in Los Angeles. I saw a productive organization staffed by some 300 people—predominantly draftsmen, keypunch operators, electric typewriter operators, woodworkers, machinists, and plastics workers. The striking fact is that 80 percent of these men and women had been unemployed only three months earlier. Disadvantaged by color, language, lack of education, or still other factors, most had been identified by the California State Employment Service as "hard core" unemployed—persons long without continuing regular jobs and without much chance of getting worthwhile employment in the ordinary course of events. A special effort of North American had put together the integrated NARTRANS staff, which recruited, guided, trained, and secured work for this group.

U.S. Secretary of Commerce C. R. Smith has said:

> Many of our most abrasive, persistent, and costly problems would disappear if people had jobs—decently paying, productive jobs, jobs with a future.

> It's as simple as that.

> Our private-enterprise economy produces and distributes more and better goods and services more efficiently and for more people than any other economic system. We now have the opportunity to bring into the system we have created a large number of Americans who up to now have been bypassed.

> We have already learned that money alone is not the remedy. In some areas members of the third generation are on relief, as were their fathers before them. Time is running out.

> We must give every American an opportunity to have the self-respect and pride which comes from individual achievement, from an honest day's work, from being no different from his self-supporting neighbor.

Many business executives with comparable beliefs have been taking active steps to make available jobs and growth opportunities to men and women who might previously have been passed by. They have been re-examining hiring standards—asking: "Why is a high school diploma 'automatically' required for this job?" and "Is this aptitude test screening out capable people because its design causes candidates of one culture to receive lower scores than those of another?" and "Why is it tacitly accepted that a person has to have a certain color or national origin to succeed on this job?" More than this, they have arranged for special recruitment techniques, for basic schooling in such areas as number skills and English, for job training, for special guidance of disadvantaged individuals not likely to have succeeded in the more usual hurly-burly of employment, and for special preparation of supervisors, managers, and others who are to work with these people.

The long-term unemployed live not only in cities but also in rural locations. The present publication illustrates particularly the efforts of industry to provide new jobs for the disadvantaged in urban areas. It reports on an AMA study undertaken to examine the approaches used by more than 40 companies employing the hard-core unemployed. The intent of this research has been to see what successes or failures are being experienced, to identify pitfalls, and to see how problems are being met.

 LAWRENCE A. JOHNSON, who conducted the study and drafted this report, is an Assistant Dean in the School of Business Administration at the University of Massachusetts. Professor Johnson has also taught at Arkansas AM&N College, North Carolina College, and San Francisco State College. He is a contributing author to several books, including *Black Capitalism* (published by the American Assembly) and *The U.S. Negro* (Stanford Research Institute). He received his Bachelor's and Master's degrees from Boston University. Portions of this study will be used as background for a Ph.D. dissertation that Professor Johnson is completing for the Stanford University Graduate School of Business.

JOHN W. ENELL
Vice President for Research

Contents

Exhibits

1. Highlights for Management

THIS STUDY was undertaken to find out what industry is doing to recruit, train, and retain the hard-core unemployed, to report the most successful methods, and also to discover how these company efforts are being perceived by residents of the urban ghettos.

The term "hard-core unemployed" has been shortened by almost everyone to "hard core" and is often used as a synonym for "minority group" or "black." The long-term unemployed resent the hard-core label. They feel that they are victims of a repressive social system and should not bear additional insults. A few companies, sensing this, take precautions to avoid placing their hard-core trainees into situations where they may inadvertently be forced to suffer the negative connotations of this label. The hard-core unemployed are men and women, endowed with a capacity for moral choice, searching for their manhood and womanhood and in their own way groping for the same truth, the same reality, the same dream and identity as all the rest of us.

A few companies have been active for years in employing and training the hard core. Even with systematic planning, however, they found that they had to learn some unexpected lessons the hard way. The majority of companies are still too new in this task to have produced tried-and-tested methods for success. As a result, the conclusions of this report rest on the practices of a relatively small sample of companies. Discussions of the pitfalls in a hard-core program are based on a much wider sample of experiences and false starts.

Companies that have launched training programs for the hard core have done so either because their chief executives believe they should do it or because of prodding by the Federal Government. Sometimes the motive was a mixture. More than once during interview visits to companies, I discovered that an executive group had been coached to a decision as a result of Government leadership.

Without this stimulus it was difficult for many businessmen to develop a rationale involving a commitment to action.

THE CRUCIAL ROLE OF THE COMPANY PRESIDENT

C. L. Hardy, president of Joseph T. Ryerson & Sons, Inc., a subsidiary of Inland Steel, pointed out that, unless the president gets involved, a hard-core training program may very well fail in its objectives: "The involvement has to be more than just a letter or a speech about the program. The message must be communicated to the frontline supervisor, and it must be communicated regularly."

The first problem that a company faces is justification of a program. Most companies are not willing to accept the fact that failure to do something now may in the long run cost the firm a great deal. Most companies still think entirely in terms of return on investment measured over a relatively short time period. Managers are evaluated on the results they produce today, this week, this month, this year. Stockholders evaluate companies in very short time cycles.

It is important that this hurdle be cleared right at the beginning. Successful efforts begin with a genuine commitment from the top. Such a commitment was made by Henry Ford II, who took on the chairmanship of the National Alliance of Businessmen (NAB) at the request of President Johnson (the NAB is now headed by Donald M. Kendall, president of Pepsico, Inc.) and undertook the task of setting up the hard-core program. Ford then appealed to and received the help of executives from major companies throughout the country. Ford not only donated a year of his own time to the effort but brought into the NAB staff another Ford executive, Leo C. Beebe, a Ford vice president, who became vice chairman of the Alliance.

Furthermore, the success of the Ford Motor Company's inner city program resulted largely from the personal interest and follow-up of Arjay Miller, then president of Ford.

Arjay Miller had asked for a weekly report on the hard-core program. The executive responsible for supplying the information to the president every Monday suggested to him by way of a memo that it might be just as valuable to have the reports monthly. The memo never reached Miller, so the executive, assuming that silence meant consent, put the new reporting period into action.

The following Monday he received a call asking that he report to the president. When asked about the hard-core report, he said that, not having had a reply to his memo, he had assumed that his suggestion had been adopted. Miller informed the executive that the weekly reports were to be continued until he was informed to the contrary. The executive's discussion of this embarrassing incident with others in the hard-core program served as a direct communiqué to all who were associated with the program that it was being watched over, very carefully, by top management.

This involvement was meaningful in that top management allowed the executive to direct the program, but let it be known that it had more than an idle interest. As Miller knew, what is not inspected often does not get done. Furthermore, the frequency of inspection has much to do with the establishment of priorities all the way down the line.

There are a thousand ways in which an employee can sense whether his superior's commitment is genuine. If there is any hesitation in the commitment, people may give up and accept failure when a program runs into difficulties.

One of the crucial decisions the president must make is how far the normal tolerances may be stretched to accommodate the hard-core programs. If every supervisor is expected to meet the tight daily and weekly quotas of production, with no loss in quality, while bringing the hard core onto the production line, support for "the president's program" may be at best tenuous and uneasy. Only the chief executive, by word and deed, can create the climate throughout the company that makes room for innovation, that spells out fair play for all concerned, and that makes the difference between token efforts and challenging commitment.

One of the most important decisions the chief executive makes is how to organize the program once the decision has been made to go ahead. By far the most common practice has been to place the direction of the program under a single executive so that at least one person will be giving full-time attention to planning, directing, coordinating, and follow-up efforts. In the case of the Ford Motor Company, Lawrence Washington, industrial relations manager at Ford's Dearborn iron foundry, was assigned to coordinate the inner city hiring program. A college graduate, and black, Washington had been employed in the Rouge plant for something like 29 years. He was moved

Author's Statement

In a large industrial company in the East, I interviewed several
executives, supervisors, staff specialists, and trainees in the company's hard-core program. All of the surface appearances were
solid. Separate facilities had been established for training. There
seemed to be a full crew of instructors, counselors, even a trained
psychologist. The hard-core program was financed in part by
Federal funds. The company held several large Government contracts. In the past year this company had placed 47 hard-core
trainees into productive jobs, the majority of them in its own
plants. It is one of those appealing statistics that you read in the
business press every week. But the disturbing fact was that the
company had a payroll of better than 20,000 people. There were
many openings in its main plant that could have been readily
filled by trainees classified as hard-core unemployed. I left this
company with a feeling that its hard-core training effort was
tokenism at its worst. After much discussion with the planners,
designers, and directors of the program in that company, I concluded that the whole thing was merely an effort to satisfy a Government agency.

In a medium-size Midwestern industrial company, I began my
interviews with the vice president for personnel. After some mild
discussion I was passed along to a young man, a recent MBA, who
had been given charge of the company's hard-core program. The
interview had hardly begun when I noticed the word "boy"
coming out when he described particular workers. Out of curiosity
I began to make a tally of how many times he used the word. By
the time we had decided to go into the plant he had said "boy"
or "boys" 19 times in referring to the hard-core trainees. The first
trainee I was introduced to told me he was 36 when I asked him
his age. I met a total of 15 men, none of whom was under 27;
one was 42. Later, as I concluded the interview with the program
director in his office, he used the word "boy" three additional
times. I asked him his age. He said he was 22.

These were two of the events that drove home the message that
there is still a big job to be done. Although in recent years there
has been no shortage of programs for the poor, there has been a

shortage of useful results. In certain ways it is clear that many individual hard-core training programs are suffering because the nation as a whole has not yet decided to do the entire job. The partial success of these hard-core training programs can be only tentative and speculative until companies across America take their share of leadership in making honest efforts to eliminate the discrimination that is so largely responsible for the economic plight of America's nonwhite population. This discrimination begins many years before the worker enters the workforce: in schools, where he or she is denied a fair chance at gaining the skills or the knowledge needed to compete in the industrial marketplace; in the communications media, where images are portrayed and aspiration levels indicated. And it continues in the plants and offices of industrial America, where the brutal or subtle forms of discrimination discourage or reject outright the nonwhite applicant.

No program in America will succeed in eliminating poverty, unemployment, or racial tensions that does not first address itself to the elimination of the fundamental causes of these problems. To beat at the branches is futile. America must begin the painful task of destroying the diseased roots that produce the bitter fruit of poverty.

For those Americans who have already been crippled by the system, American business is faced with the task of (1) providing the motivation and skill training—and the opportunities—that will enable them to join the mainstream of America's industrial world, (2) offering the opportunity to advance up the employment ladder, (3) providing the counseling and the supplementary support that will keep them from dropping out. Costly and painful experience urges that any new program designed to eradicate hard-core poverty must undertake nothing less than the whole job if it is to avoid the failure of its predecessor programs.

The decision makers in management, the men who actually turn the bolts and oil the parts—who make it go—have not yet in any widespread sense really become involved in the search for solutions to these illnesses in American society. But they are slowly coming to realize that no part of a society can long remain aloof from the pain of any other part.

to the Dearborn corporate headquarters—to the wage and manpower planning department of the labor relations staff, which would have overall responsibility for the program, and through whom Washington would report.

Like Miller at Ford, other company presidents have taken a strong personal interest in the decision who will carry out the program because they know that this is one of the strongest ways they have of getting a message communicated to the company and to the community. If the program is placed under the direction of someone who really knows what he is doing, and who has a reputation for getting things done, the whole workforce will realize quickly that the president's interest is sincere. Where companies have placed hard-core programs under inexperienced, recent college graduates, there has often been a history of half-heartedness and downright failure, no matter how well motivated the young directors were. In the appointment, everyone read what he thought was the president's intent, no matter what the speeches said.

Hard-core programs are usually placed under the authority of the personnel or the industrial relations department. This may be a mistake. Personnel executives almost always have been solidly oriented toward protecting the company from anyone whose employment might create the slightest harm to it. They have been taught to screen out, not to "screen in." They carry in their heads high standards by which to measure the people they will approve for employment.

Then everything changes 180° and the personnel executive usually has a hard time adjusting to the new way of life. What complicates the matter is that hardly any president communicates the charter to recruit hard core in such clear language that all possible ambiguities fall away. A decision is made. There is a discussion about it. Everyone agrees to go ahead. But no one dares ask whether the program is to endure only until the blacks stop raising hell, or until the urban crisis is over, or whether a genuinely new way of life is being launched, a permanent change in basic criteria. In all the companies studied everyone seemed to be feeling his way, in this sense. No company has yet spelled out a real timetable, or has yet spoken out clearly one way or another on this question of endurance.

So the personnel executive tends to hedge his bets. Often he tries to protect himself by going after the "cleanest" of the hard core, those who are most likely to work out satisfactorily, and not attempt to

Basis of the Research

The information that is the basis of this study, and the company materials that illustrate some of the practices used in employing the hard-core unemployed, were developed from interviews with executives, foremen, staff specialists, and employees of 43 companies across the United States. The companies represent industrial, retail, and service types of operations, some employing less than 100 workers, others employing tens of thousands. Interviews were also conducted with residents of the ghettos of Boston, Detroit, Los Angeles, and San Francisco.

From June 1968 to January 1969 the author made personal visits to the companies to conduct the interviews. In April and May 1969 he updated the research data on which important conclusions would be based to include the latest information.

The results of the research do not permit categorical statements about the perfect model for hiring and training the hard core. However, some companies have overcome difficult problems and have developed useful approaches.

Exhibit materials and quoted comments in this report are used with the permission of the individuals and the companies concerned.

foment revolutions. Many of these hard core from the top layers have already been hired and employed. Increasingly, hard-core hiring will be dipping into more difficult layers. Any company that is going to really dig will have to set up clear policies, clear objectives, and clear criteria for measurement. Otherwise, its executives may become very uneasy.

Although urban affairs departments are beginning to spring up like mushrooms, there is no evidence yet that companies are coordinating their hard-core training programs with their urban affairs efforts. The reason may be that the hard-core programs usually are nurtured in the personnel departments, and the urban affairs programs in the public relations departments. Historically, these departments have not closely coordinated their missions.

The president also has to make basic decisions about funding hard-core programs. Some companies, such as General Motors, have chosen to go the whole way alone without any Government financial aid. Other companies have chosen to achieve virtually a 100 percent Government subsidiary for their programs. Many companies take a halfway approach, basing their applications for Government support on the degree of effort involved but bearing a major or minor portion of the costs themselves.

Surprisingly, the companies that have launched hard-core programs usually did not make any special effort to coach their foremen in advance about the modifications that would be expected in the foremen's role. In practically every company with a hard-core program, however, efforts to sensitize, orient, create awareness of the hard core, and so forth were begun rather quickly when problems developed. At the moment, sensitivity training for foremen (under many labels) is receiving extraordinary attention.

No company in the survey made special efforts to "prepare" the workforce for receiving the hard core. Much the opposite. Because of the stigma attached to the hard-core label, companies are trying their best to make the training and job placement of the hard core as much a part of ordinary work processes as possible, to make the extraordinary seem ordinary.

Companies that have succeeded have recognized that good intentions, noble ideals, or Government pressure are not enough to get the job done. Planning is essential. Realistic objectives are essential. Company experiences show that the chief executive must make it crystal-clear that he backs the hard-core training fully and will set up check points to monitor progress toward planned objectives. Anything less than this will weaken the program from the start. The variables are already complex, and many of the people involved will need encouragement. This point cannot be overemphasized: Top management must be totally committed, and this commitment must be expressed in actions as well as words. Many presidents have stated this position without equivocation. They know that employees at all levels take their cues from the executive's behavior, not his speeches.

One of the executives who was interviewed offered this advice:

Plan, plan, plan, and you will avoid the many problems that beset most new programs. Make sure a job exists before you begin beating the drum for recruits. Make sure the job is meaningful and lacks the stigma attached to low-paying and low-prestige tasks. Try to project a career-ladder type of job and keep the ladder open and available. Above all, do not oversell the type of job, the amount of pay, or the opportunities. This can backfire and be embarrassing. Pay is important, especially the initial pay checks. Have them on time and correct.

This advice seems pertinent; yet even firm commitment on the part of senior management cannot prevent some minor frustration such as that experienced in the program conducted by Lockheed-Georgia Company, a division of Lockheed Aircraft Corporation. The hard-core program was well conceived and well operated, and produced young men who were qualified for jobs and were ready to begin working. Openings did not develop in sufficient quantity at Lockheed-Georgia, however, and the training center found it necessary to place the trained hard core with other employers in the area. Although all the trainees received jobs, they expressed feelings of disappointment in that they had anticipated working for Lockheed, which carries a degree of prestige in their locality.

UNION SUPPORT IS USUALLY NECESSARY

The role of labor unions in hard-core programs was not within the scope of this study; however, a brief exploration of union attitudes was planned, and toward that purpose I spoke with a few top union leaders. While they expressed a willingness to cooperate in these programs, they are keenly aware of the fears that concern some of their members. They also pointed out that it is essential to bring the union into consultation during the planning phases of a hard-core program.

When hard core are introduced into a plant, it is often necessary to make certain exceptions to the rules that might exist in a union contract, such as those applying to membership in a union or an apprenticeship, internship history, or employment tests.

Some unions still bar minorities from membership, severely restrict apprenticeships, and often block the advancement of the few minority members admitted. The union membership might leave such decisions to the union officials, trusting them to protect the members. The more subtle and therefore more difficult task faced by the union leadership is that of avoiding a white backlash that might set in and defeat any hard-core program.

A leadership that has been closely associated in a meaningful way with civil rights programs or minority activities will perhaps have an easier task. One of the labor leaders who have been very closely identified with such activities is Walter Reuther, of the United Auto Workers. It is likely that his efforts in this area contributed to the early introduction of hard-core programs into various automotive plants throughout the country.

In this discussion of leadership it should be understood that the rank and file tend to pay very little attention to directives unless those directives are clearly to their benefit or are of major significance to them. Union members have been conditioned to expect and accept certain programs from their leadership. The attitudes and behavior of the leadership are usually reflected in union publications or are reported in the daily press. The response of a union membership may be difficult, if not impossible, to measure. Unless the leadership behavior is in some way threatening to the ranks of the membership, there may be no response. This should not be interpreted as approval. A positive attitude by a labor leader may have some effect on the membership, but there is no known study that attempts such correlation.

A further complication of recent development is that a group of black militants employed in the auto industry is challenging the right of the United Auto Workers to represent Negro workers. To the extent that this militancy continues, its effect on union participation in the hard-core programs cannot yet be anticipated.

GUIDELINES FOR PROCEEDING

The author's observations and many interviews have gradually sketched a picture of the company practices most generally associated with productive projects for the employment of the hard core. Briefly, these findings are that—

1. It is possible to recruit the hard-core unemployed. Magazines and newspapers may not be the best vehicles. Radio ads on "soul" stations work best. Companies that have achieved success have sent representatives into the ghettos to recruit. The hard core have been so long shunned by society that they are deeply suspicious of the sincerity of virtually all employers. They have to be convinced.

2. Planning and organizing a hard-core employment program should never be done casually, no matter how small the effort. Explosive emotions are usually involved. New behavior patterns must be established very quickly—the hard core need to become more "industrialized," the supervisors more "sensitized." Companies that have tackled these programs successfully have set realistic objectives. Some have brought the "line" organizations in at an early stage so that the program would not be resisted in the belief that it sprang full-blown as the brainchild of another department. Others have established the hard-core training in such a way that the "line" never knew that it was receiving hard core in the work crews. The successful companies have also made sure that jobs were waiting at the end of the training period.

3. When a recruiting effort is being organized, clear definitions of "hard core" are necessary for the recruiters. Otherwise, only the "cleanest" of the hard core may be hired, or the recruitment effort may yield ghetto residents simply looking for a chance for better jobs than they already have.

4. Black "pimps" should be avoided—those who try to represent the black community to employers and in the process pick the pockets of both the employers and the long-term unemployed. Companies with successful recruitment programs work with legitimate agencies in the ghettos, such as the United States Employment Service, Department of Labor.

5. Although sensitivity training for personnel in the employment office has not yet been attempted to any degree, there may be merit in such an approach. Employment personnel not only must adapt themselves quickly to the new type of recruit, but also have to create a friendly, receptive atmosphere in the employment office because the whole scene is so strange and alien to the hard-core people recruited.

6. Successful interviews with the hard core are accomplished on a formal, last-name basis, in a low key. A careful interviewer does not talk about all other blacks as if they were universally bright, or his

"best" friends. Other mannerisms that may be regarded as condescending, or sarcastic, also should be avoided. If the employment application form is not simplified, the hard core may need help in filling it out. Hiring a black interviewer is no guarantee, companies have found, that communication with other blacks will take place. There is much emotion within the black community right now about the proper norms for black-white relationships.

7. To get the hard core past the employment office, companies have to modify or eliminate many of the normal procedures. These include retail credit checks, high school degrees or other educational requirements, certain physical standards, and automatic disqualification because of a record of arrests or convictions. Tests, if used at all, should be administered only to establish the level of training required. But the hard core must be persuaded that the tests are not being used to disqualify them. Many companies are finding that much of the testing that is normally done has little relevance to the requirements of the work to be performed.

8. Anything short of scrupulous honesty in describing jobs and future job opportunities is likely to backfire. The prospect of mobility is essential to many of the hard core.

9. The trainees must draw a living wage as soon as they come into the program. They may be attempting to escape the welfare rolls and need enough money to replace the dole. Many of the hard core have families to support.

10. Although most companies have made no attempt to stay away from the classroom atmosphere for their hard-core training, it is probably advisable that companies create this atmosphere with utmost caution. This is the atmosphere that is synonymous with failure in the opinion of most of the hard core. Small classes help, where individual attention can be given to each trainee. Training the hard core can take as much as three to four times longer than training regular employees. Training must be conducted in a businesslike manner, standards must be set and maintained, and good work habits should be established early. Black instructors may be more effective than white because they can bear down on disciplinary problems without touching on so many automatically sensitive areas. In the initial stages of the program discipline must be used sympathetically in the main problem area companies have faced—tardiness and absence. Since this problem is closely correlated with inadequate transportation

facilities, companies must be prepared to offer extraordinary help in the beginning, such as establishing a bus service or towing a car off a freeway. They may even find themselves bailing someone out of jail.

11. Some hard core, particularly many of those hired in the earliest programs, can perform industrial jobs easily with a minimum of instruction; in fact, they have often become very angry on seeing how simple the jobs were that had been denied them so long. Most of the hard core, however, will need fundamental education as well as instructions and help in such matters as credit buying, budgeting, and nutrition. The "buddy system" has become popular as a means of providing individual attention in areas that do not require specialized knowledge.

12. Job-skills training should focus on specific jobs, and all instructions should be clearcut in every detail. Procedures should be broken down into their simplest components for ease of communication to the hard core. The rule is, stay specific. If there is no procedure for a task, develop one.

It is helpful to set the training standards slightly higher than those that will be required by the line organizations. This will help when the trainee enters a regular work crew. Training programs are more effective if they allow for exposure to the noise and hustle of the plant. When a trainee is suddenly placed into the plant without the benefit of previous exposure, his disorientation may last for several days.

13. It is doubtful that the sensitizing sessions that some companies are using with their hard-core trainees are having the desired effect. The trainees dislike being sensitized to establishment attitudes. They respond most quickly to training for specific jobs, and in specific skills.

14. Some companies have found that, unless precautions are taken, a few supervisors will emerge from sensitivity training with too much empathy for the hard core and, in a response desired by neither the companies nor the hard core, will begin to accept inferior levels of performance. Executives emphasize that performance standards must be maintained.

15. Effective supervisory training emphasizes that the hard core will involve the supervisors in a "total" relationship, coming to them for counsel in many personal matters, and sometimes for small loans. Candor and honesty are the basic ingredients required in this rela-

tionship. But before such a relationship can develop, the hard core will test the supervisors repeatedly to discover whether their attitudes are genuine. (The same applies with instructors.) It may be helpful to explore in advance with the supervisors the kinds of situations they may confront in working with the hard core and to help them develop effective patterns of response.

16. The original concept of sensitivity training is wearing many faces these days and has become very popular for coaching supervisors and others involved in hard-core programs. But, as one company emphasizes, the goal should not necessarily be to change attitudes, but rather to change behavior when that is necessary.

17. Under the banner of sensitivity training, at least one company plunged its supervisors into a head-on confrontation with black militants from the ghetto to achieve a dialogue. It took about six months to get the program back on the tracks.

18. Placing a hard-core trainee in a regular work crew doesn't mean the job is over. Companies that have been through more than one cycle of training have found that follow-up is necessary to help with posttraining problems, such as a belief that the supervisor is a racist.

19. Probably no company should train the hard-core unemployed unless it can offer meaningful, permanent jobs at the end of the program. The jobs must be the kind men can talk about when they go back into their neighborhoods. Among the hard core there is a deep stigma attached to janitorial work.

20. Residents of the urban ghettos, to whom these programs are addressed, view them with mixed reactions. Many of these people are still not convinced that American industry has really achieved an about-face. They would not be surprised if these hard-core training programs were to come to an end tomorrow. Others are simply happy to have a job, to be working and supporting themselves and their families. Many of the "hardest" hard core have never yet been reached by company recruiting programs and don't care to be. The young blacks are very angry. They still feel in overwhelming numbers that too little is being done, and too late. Only the relatively small number of companies that have established their credentials among these young men, by employing blacks before the pressure of the civil rights movement began, or Government persuasion began, or those employing blacks in highly skilled positions and in the executive suite have yet bridged the great gulf separating the two societies.

EXHIBIT 1. *Statement by the Chief Executive Officer of Xerox Corporation to All Xerox Managers*

XEROX

The Xerox Manager

Interpretive Information for Xerox Managers

Number 12
May 2, 1968

To All Xerox Managers:

We at Xerox are among those who are compelled to accept the indictment of the National Advisory Commission on Civil Disorders: "What white Americans have never fully understood -- but what the Negro can never forget -- is that white society is deeply implicated in the ghetto. White institutions created it, white institutions maintain it, and white society condones it."

We, like all other Americans, share the responsibility for a color-divided nation; and in all honesty, we need not look beyond our own doorstep to find out why.

In Rochester, one of the first American cities scarred by racial strife, Xerox continues to employ only a very small percentage of Negroes. In other major cities, including some that have suffered even greater violence, we employ no Negroes at all.

Thus, despite a stated policy that seeks to fulfill our obligations to society -- and even though the significant steps we have taken have been publicly praised -- our performance is still far from a shining beacon of corporate responsibility.

We know, of course, that many Negroes - fearing rejection - simply don't apply to Xerox for jobs. And of those who do apply, many fail to meet our usual standards of qualification. But those factors obviously cannot be used as excuses. They are, rather, the very problems which Xerox must and will attack in the future.

In order to respond with concerted action to the Advisory Commission's recommendations that American industry hire, train and suitably employ one million Negroes within the next three years, we are therefore going to adopt these immediate courses of action:

Exhibit 1 (continued)

First, <u>we will heavily intensify our recruiting of Negroes</u>
and other minorities. If, as our past experience indicates,
they are reluctant to come to us, then we will go to them.

A special recruiting effort at University Microfilms in
Ann Arbor, Michigan has proved the validity of this approach
by substantially increasing minority employment in the space
of a few months. We will now extend that effort throughout
all the departments, divisions, and subsidiaries of Xerox.

Secondly, <u>all managers responsible for hiring -- regardless
of geographical location -- will re-examine their selection
standards and training programs.</u> Our past efforts, by and
large, have sought to find only the "best qualified" people
for Xerox, regardless of age, race or religion. But that
goal, however valid, has inadvertently excluded many good
people from productive employment.

We are, accordingly, going to change the selection standards
that screen out all but the most qualified people. We will
also begin devoting special attention to minority employees
of limited qualifications to make them genuinely productive
in the shortest possible time. Hopefully we can maintain
standards of performance throughout.

Effective immediately, therefore, all Xerox managers are
directed, on an individual basis, to begin this effort, pending a more systematic company-wide revision of standards.

Thirdly, <u>we are planning to increase substantially our training of unqualified Negroes, and other minority members.</u>

Although the Project Step Up Program to qualify people for
"entry level" jobs has been successful in the Rochester area,
we feel that its scope must be considerably broadened and the
entry requirements modified. We are presently planning to
incorporate the program into our present hiring process, and
to extend it to major Xerox facilities outside Rochester.

The full and unqualified cooperation of all Xerox managers
is expected in reaching our minority hiring goals. Corporate
Personnel has been given the responsibility for implementing
our plans, and for establishing an accountability system
through which top management -- beginning immediately -- can
regularly assess progress in all divisions, departments and
subsidiaries of the corporation.

Exhibit 1 (concluded)

Today there are 22 million Negroes in the United States.
The exclusion of many of them from our society is a malig-
nancy that the nation cannot endure. To include them as
integral to the nation, however, will mean even more than
the correction of an intolerable injustice. It will also
mean the creation of an enormous and affluent market for
new products and services, and of an equally enormous pool
of manpower to help meet the critical shortages predicted
for the future.

We are fully aware, of course, of the progress that Xerox
has already made in assisting the civil rights movement.

But it simply has not gone far enough.

We must do more because Xerox will not add to the misery of
the present condition of most Negroes. It will not condone
the waste of a great national resource. It will not compromise the conviction on which the success of this enterprise
and of the nation depends.

EXHIBIT 2. *"Developing Plans for Helping New Hourly Employees Succeed on the Job," a Description of Ford Motor Company's Planning Effort*

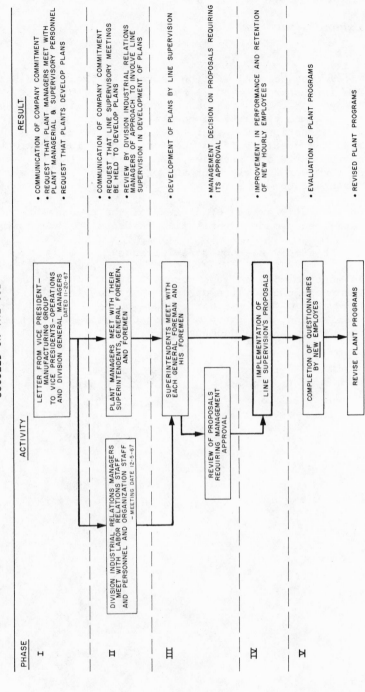

DEVELOPING PLANS FOR
HELPING NEW HOURLY EMPLOYEES
SUCCEED ON THE JOB

PHASE

ACTIVITY

RESULT

I

LETTER FROM VICE PRESIDENT—
MANUFACTURING GROUP
TO VICE PRESIDENTS–OPERATIONS
AND DIVISION GENERAL MANAGERS
DATED 11-20-67

- COMMUNICATION OF COMPANY COMMITMENT
- REQUEST THAT PLANT MANAGERS MEET WITH PLANT MANAGERIAL & SUPERVISORY PERSONNEL
- REQUEST THAT PLANTS DEVELOP PLANS

II

DIVISION INDUSTRIAL RELATIONS MANAGERS
MEET WITH LABOR RELATIONS STAFF
AND PERSONNEL AND ORGANIZATION STAFF
— MEETING DATE 12-5-67

PLANT MANAGERS MEET WITH THEIR
SUPERINTENDENTS, GENERAL FOREMEN,
AND FOREMEN

- COMMUNICATION OF COMPANY COMMITMENT
- REQUEST THAT LINE SUPERVISORY MEETINGS BE HELD TO DEVELOP PLANS
- REVIEW BY DIVISION INDUSTRIAL RELATIONS MANAGERS OF APPROACH TO INVOLVE LINE SUPERVISION IN DEVELOPMENT OF PLANS

III

SUPERINTENDENTS MEET WITH
EACH GENERAL FOREMAN AND
HIS FOREMEN

REVIEW OF PROPOSALS
REQUIRING MANAGEMENT
APPROVAL

- DEVELOPMENT OF PLANS BY LINE SUPERVISION

- MANAGEMENT DECISION ON PROPOSALS REQUIRING ITS APPROVAL

IV

IMPLEMENTATION OF
LINE SUPERVISION'S PROPOSALS

- IMPROVEMENT IN PERFORMANCE AND RETENTION OF NEW HOURLY EMPLOYEES

V

COMPLETION OF QUESTIONNAIRES
BY NEW EMPLOYES

REVISE PLANT PROGRAMS

- EVALUATION OF PLANT PROGRAMS

- REVISED PLANT PROGRAMS

EXHIBIT 3. *Proposed Lockheed Hard-Core Hiring Program*

PROPOSED LOCKHEED "HARD CORE" HIRING PROGRAM

<u>Objective</u>: To hire a substantial number of "hard core" un-
employed, keep track of their progress, learn
"how" to use this manpower source and, if experience warrants, share our findings with others.

<u>Definitions</u>:
1. A "hard core" unemployed person is one who
   a. Has been unemployed for most of the past year.
   b. Has had no, or an unstable, work record during
      the past five years.
   c. Is disadvantaged or economically deprived.
      Roughly, this would include a person whose yearly
      income is, and has been, $3,000 or less.
   d. Is a school (elementary, junior high, or high
      school) dropout.
   In addition, it is desired that among the hard-core
   group hired
   a. At least 75 percent be members of a minority
      (Negro or Mexican-American) group.
   b. At least 25 percent have police records, not to
      include convictions for major crimes.
2. <u>Substantial</u> relates to number, time, and status of
   persons involved. For the purpose of this program, it
   is defined as 1 percent of the average hourly workforce or 5 percent of the hourly hires, whichever is
   less, during a calendar year, and relates to persons
   included in an identifiable program not to exceed one
   year in length.

<u>Implementation</u>:
<u>Schedule</u>
The program will begin 1 January 1967.

<u>Reports</u>
The requirement for program reports will be held in
abeyance, pending determination of other aspects of the
program.

Exhibit 3 (concluded)

Recruiting/Selection

Subject to the criteria discussed above under "Definitions," probably the most important factor to be considered in the selection of candidates for this program is
whether they can be motivated and, as a corollary,
trained.

A basic test battery should be developed and given to
maximize selection success and to correlate success with
specific test patterns. Tests should be designed to determine those who are "qualifiable," rather than "qualified."
They should not be designed primarily to "exclude," but
to carry out the intent of the program; that is, the
hire and assimilation into the workforce of "hard core"
unemployed persons. Particular attention should be given
to nonverbal learning ability.

Careful attention should be given in reviewing criminal
or police records; convictions, not arrests or charges,
are what count. Consideration should be given to the
nature of the crime, how long ago it occurred, age of the
person at the time of its commission, circumstances pre-
vailing, and any evidence of the establishment and maintenance of an adverse-conduct pattern.

Types of Entry-Level Jobs or Occupations

Where possible, entry-level occupations used for hire
should be those that
1. Impose modest demands and are of a nature to whet,
   so to speak, the candidates' appetites.
2. Present a path for advancement.

Indoctrination/Control

It is desired that this program be handled in a manner
analogous to a controlled laboratory experiment. Special
orientation sessions should be planned and conducted. The
individual progress of employees in this program should
be carefully tracked and records kept.

2. Who Are the Hard-Core Unemployed?

THE FAILURE of our economy and society to provide equal job opportunities for all is not the only contributory factor, but is a key variable in the perpetuation of the tinderbox on which America sits. Discrimination, inadequate education, and lack of industrial experience have created in urban America a large pool of people, mostly black, who constitute a group labeled, for lack of a better term, "hard-core unemployed." It is unfair to generalize about this group except to say that they are poor and unemployed, and have been for some time. They find it difficult to qualify for most jobs; and, when they work, they do so in the low-skill, low-paying occupations.

Among the companies surveyed for this research report there was no general agreement about the definition of "hard-core unemployed." As a result, some companies have recruited and built training and counseling programs around groups that were simply black and underemployed, then wondered what the fuss was all about.

In general, the lack of clear definitions tends to fix the sights of recruiters on the "acceptable" hard core, those who are not too different. Every company seems to want to do its bit; only it is apparent that executives don't want their problems in large doses, so it is likely that the hard core within the hard core will remain apart from industrial employment.

The most widespread definition is the one used by the U.S. Department of Labor, particularly to test situations in which money subsidies will be granted to companies that begin hard-core programs. This definition calls for hard core to be unemployed and poor, plus any one of the following:

- Under 22.
- Over 45.
- Handicapped.

- School dropout.
- Subject to special obstacles to employment.

Government representatives, in briefing businessmen on hard-core programs, often use the term "minority group" as a synonym for the last factor, although a number of other considerations are actually listed. "Minority group" is defined as Negroes, American-Indians, Japanese, Chinese, Filipinos, Koreans, Polynesians, Indonesians, Hawaiians, Aleuts, Eskimos, Mexican-Americans, Puerto Ricans, and other people with Spanish surnames.

The National Alliance of Businessmen further describes the profile of a typical hard-core trainee as follows (these facts were confirmed in my interviews with hard core in the urban ghettos):

- Unemployed for at least 18 months.
- Never received any intensive skill training.
- Parents were unskilled.
- Needs eyeglasses and dental help right away.
- No transportation facilities.
- Sixth-grade education.
- Has seen a doctor only once in his life.
- Lives with one and a half families.
- Some previous scrape with the law; spent at least 30 days in jail.
- Is married, has three children.

Though Negroes constitute approximately 11 percent of the nation's workforce, they account for over 20 percent of the unemployed, according to latest Labor Department statistics. It is true that efforts are being made to alleviate the situation and that jobs are opening up in areas that were previously closed, but this does not alter the situation of Negro workers as a whole. The bulk of the Negro labor pool is unskilled, and the marketplace is becoming more technical with each passing day; thus the problem is compounded for the unequipped black worker.

Blacks do not, however, have a monopoly or exclusive rights to the word "hard core." The face of the uneducated, unskilled, and thus unemployed is multicolored. It is black, brown, red, yellow, and white. The language is multilingual. Every major city in the United

States has large numbers of hard core. The Puerto Ricans dominate East Harlem and are becoming numerous in Harlem proper. Mexican-Americans are by far the largest group of hard core in San Antonio, and many live in southern California cities and in Phoenix, Arizona. There are contingents of whites, former farm workers, living in the slums of St. Louis, Chicago, San Francisco, and other cities.

Segmenting the Hard Core

It is important to categorize the people who are thought of as hard-core unemployed. Though it is difficult to draw nice clean lines, it is necessary to attempt a distinction. Differences, though often subtle, do exist. Management will not be dealing with a homogeneous group of workers who all think alike and therefore can be expected to respond to common stimuli. Age, education, place of birth, attitudes toward work and authority, and the mere tempo of the times will have a great influence on the responses one can expect. But these responses will differ depending on the group involved.

There are first the young blacks born in the urban centers of the North, rebellious, angry, and terribly insecure. They have quit school, lack any marketable skills, and have by and large given up on the "system" as the instrument to solve their problems.

Second, there are older men and women (45 and above) who have dwelt in the cities most of their adult lives. They were attracted to the northern industrial centers to work in the defense plants: tanks and trucks in the Detroit complex, planes and ships along the West Coast, guns and clothing in the East. Most of their jobs ended with the War, but they chose to remain. Though they had acquired some industrial experience, they lacked the seniority or union support that would permit a transition to civilian jobs.

Third, there are the new migrants who came into the northern cities at an alarming rate until between 1966 and 1968. Although this massive migration has now begun to decline, the migrants who have already come north swell the unemployment rolls. They came from rural backgrounds, from the unproductive farms of Mississippi, Louisiana, Alabama, and Arkansas. They came out of the hill country of Virginia and Georgia. They fled the mechanization of the huge plantations of the South. They, too, are uneducated, without industrial skills, and totally unsophisticated about the ways of urban life.

Fourth, there are the Puerto Ricans, who have settled by and large in the Northeast. In addition to the educational gap, they carry the burden of a language problem. Money is their primary goal, and they quit school as soon as it is legally possible in order to seek work. They compete aggressively with the Negro for the most menial job. They also face, perhaps to an even greater degree than the Negro, the problem of discrimination in employment.

Fifth, the Mexican-American, who usually lives in the Southwest and is by and large nonmobile. He is poorly educated, limited in industrial skills, and restricted, because of discrimination, to agricultural types of employment.

Sixth and last, the American Indian. Very little is known about this group of people, who exist in virtual exile from the mainstream of American life. But they are by definition part of the hard core, and a program is under way in Madera, California, to train and incorporate them into the economy.

These six groups have enough in common to fit under one label, but differ enough in their experiences to require an understanding of these differences before attempts are made to recruit, train, or place them in a job setting.

THE YOUNG BLACKS

The most striking population change affecting the central cities is the rapid increase of the Negro population and the shift of the white population to the suburbs. The Negro population in all central cities taken together increased by 20 percent between 1960 and 1965, while the white population there actually declined (for the first time, and by about 1 percent).[1] The proportion of Negroes in the central city population has more than doubled in the past quarter century. It actually increased at a faster rate between 1960 and 1965 than in

---

[1] The discussion in this section relates to "central cities" of Standard Metropolitan Statistical Areas (SMSA's include one or more counties with a central city of 50,000 or more). This group of 212 cities included an estimated population of 43.4 million people age 14 and over in April 1965.

the previous decade. Conversely, Negroes have not been able to make real entry into the suburbs. They represented only 5 percent of the suburban population in 1965, approximately the same proportion as a generation earlier.

The fact that should be of particular interest to managements, as they address themselves to the problem of the hard core, is the tremendous increase in the Negro teenage population. The number of Negro teenagers in cities rose by over 50 percent in the short five-year period 1960 to 1965—about twice as fast as the teenage population nationally. And the Negro young adult population (age 20 to 24) rose by one-fourth. These unprecedented increases in numbers of young people—many of them out of jobs, most of them out of school —serve as a potential source of social dynamite.

Frustration and disillusionment in young people can be channeled into anger as well as despair. This may generate different types of behavior—one may drop out of school, give up in the attempt to find a job, join a gang, participate in illegal forms of activity, or merely turn his back on society.

Education of young blacks. Inadequate and inferior education is obviously one of the major elements in the total subemployment problem of young people. Unable to produce a high school diploma or pass an entry-level examination, youngsters are forced into the low-skilled, low-paying jobs. In hiring workers, employers require high school diplomas, not only for white-collar jobs, but also for the apprenticeships in skilled areas or even for semiskilled jobs. Often this requirement will have little or no relevance to the task to be performed. Faced with this hurdle, which youngsters read as discrimination, many merely withdraw from the job market.

The education of black students differs quite markedly from that offered to whites. This is particularly true if the black youngster attends school in the central city. It does not matter whether he lives in the North, West, South, or Midwest of the United States. According to the Governor's Commission on the Los Angeles Riots, the city-wide school dropout rate for former ninth-grade students was 30 percent in 1965; but in three predominantly Negro high schools in south central Los Angeles, two-thirds of the student body dropped out before graduation.

Overcrowding and double sessions, prevalent in the schools in Watts and other slum areas of Los Angeles, are among the factors contributing to this record of educational failure. Over three-fourths of the 26,200 students who were on double session in the city schools in 1965 were in schools of predominantly Negro or Mexican-American enrollments. Furthermore, at that time, these schools generally lacked cafeterias, and none of the Los Angeles schools provided free or reduced-price lunches for needy children, whose school progress might have been aided by better nourishment. The schools in the city's poverty areas often lacked libraries; and, in general, the average teacher in these schools was less experienced than other teachers in the city school system as a whole.

In a recent study on students in two junior high schools in Harlem, it was found that roughly two-thirds of the students enrolled in the ninth grade failed to graduate from high school.

There is no senior high school in all of central Harlem, although there are 20 elementary schools and 4 junior high schools in the district. Thus, if a student wishes to attend high school, it is necessary for him to commute to another section of the city. Hidden in the statistics of those that make the journey and eventually receive a high school diploma is the actual gap between years of school completed and educational achievement. According to a nationwide study sponsored by the U.S. Department of Health, Education, and Welfare, covering some 4,000 schools and 645,000 children, minority children start school with a serious educational deficiency and the gap widens as they progress.[2]

The average twelfth-grade Negro in metropolitan areas, according to the report, achieves scores in mathematics that equal the average for seventh- or eighth-grade students in the country as a whole, and the record in reading is only moderately better.

Puerto Ricans and Mexican-Americans post similar records. In East Harlem, better than 40 percent of the Puerto Rican unemployed had at best reached the eighth grade in school. Sixty percent of the Mexican-American unemployed in Phoenix had never gone beyond the eighth grade, and almost 20 percent had only four years of school or less.

Attitudes of young blacks. For most people the way to a more affluent and satisfying life is through meaningful work. For this reason

[2] *Equality of Educational Opportunity*, U.S. Department of Health, Education, and Welfare, Washington, D.C., 1966, pp. 1–33.

most people spend a great deal of time, energy, and money preparing for a job; and, once the job has been obtained, they concern themselves with the problem of moving up the occupational ladder. This kind of activity consumes a large portion of most people's lives. Too little is yet known about the effects of slum life and the accompanying environment upon the aspirations and motivation of the ghetto resident. Scattered studies indicate a serious gap between his aspirations and the opportunities to realize them.

Most black youngsters do not believe that they will ever be able to secure a decent job at a decent salary—a salary that will permit them to purchase the material goods that they so desperately want. A history of job search and frustration or failure causes them to eventually lose faith in themselves and the system.

The narrowness of the job search by these young people has been documented by many studies—among them is one recently made for the Federal Government. These young men more often looked for jobs by checking newspapers ads and inquiring around among friends and relatives rather than by going directly to employing establishments or employment agencies, either public or private.[3] It is only later, after they have found that practically all the ads contain some provision that tends to exclude them, and even after that, when their few attempts to apply for jobs have met with failure, that they stop reading the ads.

The job-seeking patterns of 450 youths in Philadelphia were also examined in a recent study.[4] The most striking finding was that two-fifths of these young people had never made a single contact with an employer. Only one out of five had made as many as one such contact per week. The longer the period of their unemployment, the less effort they made to find jobs.

How little these youngsters know about jobs is shown in the high proportion (nearly one-half) who were unable to express any job pref-

---

[3] Samuel M. Myers, *The Unemployed and the Underemployed: A Study of Applicants for Laborers' Jobs,* Bureau of Social Science Research, Inc., Washington, D.C., November, 1966 (mimeographed). Submitted to the Office of Economic Opportunity.

[4] Saul S. Leshner and George S. Snyderman, *Job Seeking Patterns of Disadvantaged Youth, Preparing Disadvantaged Youth for Work,* U.S. Department of Labor, Manpower Administration, Bureau of Employment Security, Washington, D.C., 1966; reprints from *Employment Service Review,* pp. 1–3.

erences. Those who had preferences cited the jobs commonly held by friends or relatives.

The men who did make a direct contact usually applied at a factory ("because of better pay") or at a small neighborhood store ("because the larger stores require high school diplomas even for packing, delivery, stockroom, or sweeping jobs"). The girls apply to nursing homes and hospitals, despite the low wages, because these places "do not require diplomas" and they provide "free meals."

Faced with these limited alternatives, they do not look upon work as the means to secure the material things they want. They view the diploma requirement as a "dodge" on the part of the firm as a reason not to hire them. They have adopted the language of their parents— "last hired, first fired." To make it "you have to be twice as good as a white." In dealing with industry, which to them means dealing with whites, they quote the Harlem proverb: "Blessed is he who expects nothing, for he will not be disappointed." They trust no one, and this includes the black people who are now appearing in personnel offices in many firms around the country. They distrust anything and everything that they have not personally tested or that one of their "group" has not tested. They seem pretty certain that they will never "make it" by working. If pushed on this point, they use as their frame of reference their parents, whose lives have been marginal at best.

And yet they are surrounded by, and want, the material things that symbolize a good life. They desperately want the cars, the clothes, the comfortable homes, and the security of a family. But experience has taught them that the world of work leads nowhere, so many elect to remain outside and hope "to make it" by hustling—"by beating the system."

Having rejected work as a means of achieving their goals, they pursue other avenues. These pursuits are usually illegal and require entry into the world of gambling, of dealing in numbers, or pimping. But even these professions require certain skills, and those who meet with failure here may, in despair, give up their goals and all hopes of ever achieving them and succumb to drug addiction, alcohol, or vagrancy. But again, even these habits require some means of support, so the path inevitably leads to the world of theft and eventually to jail.

Having all these aspirations but lacking the ability to do anything about them tends to frustrate and shape their attitudes about work. Their environment, which is usually dirty and overpowering, proves to them "how useless it is for them to even try to move into a more socially desirable and materially rewarding position in society."[5]

This negative attitude held by the young blacks toward work and industry represents the major hurdle over which industry must jump if the recruitment, training, and employment of these young people are to be successful.

This attitude toward work and industry lies along a spectrum. Some of the young people, particularly the females, will adapt to the world of work with a minimum of effort; others will take longer to reduce the anger and distrust; and for some the conversion may never take place.

If companies can offer meaningful jobs and can make available the resources that will be needed to bring these young people along, it does not seem unrealistic to believe that many of them can be salvaged. The key lies in the employers' ability to convince these young people that they will be offered meaningful employment and that the companies will exercise the patience needed to help them become productive workers. Meaningful jobs, to these young people, are jobs above the janitorial level, or the maid level in the case of young women. The pay that accompanies these jobs must be equal to that of other employees doing the same kinds of tasks.

Behavior patterns of the young blacks. Most of the readers of this research report have at best only a second- or a third-hand knowledge of the ghetto residents—from the television screen, the daily paper, the popular news magazines, the view from the commuter train, or the rare occasion of an actual visit. Few, if any, have ever been exposed to the kind of world that these youngsters must deal with each and every day. Neither armchair research nor conversations with "knowledgeable blacks" will allow anyone to duplicate or really understand the experience of being black in America. Therefore, the dress, the slang, the hairstyles, and the behavior of the hard-core unemployed will be alien to most of the experiences in the employers'

---

[5] Alvin L. Schorr, *Slum and Social Security*, U.S. Department of Health, Education, and Welfare, Social Security Administration Division of Research and Statistics, Research Report No. 1, Washington, D.C., 1963, p. 47.

background. The Bureau of Labor Statistics has reported that "compared to whites, Negroes still are more than three times as likely to be in poverty, twice as likely to be unemployed, and three times as likely to die in infancy or childbirth." These young people may be from homes with one or more parents absent; there may be an alcoholic parent present; it is almost certain that the home has experienced, and perhaps is experiencing, severe economic problems. Just these few variables can produce a wide range of "deviant" behavior patterns. Coupling any of these with the many negative cues that black youngsters receive most of their lives, one can begin to appreciate, if not understand, the behavior.

The response must be viewed in the framework of the broader community, which, by its policies of social segregation and discrimination, has withheld from these youngsters the opportunity to achieve or to identify with a status position in the larger society. The observed behavior, then, is an adaptation to such blocking and frustration in which a segment of the population turns in upon itself and attempts to develop within itself criteria for the achievement of social status and the rudiments of a satisfactory social life.

Despite the location of their world, which is in the drabbest, most cluttered, most physically deteriorated sections of the city, many place a great emphasis upon clothing and seek expression in this manner. The suit, shirt, shoes, and accessories are so chosen that they harmonize and suggest an exquisite sense of taste. In addition to clothing, great store is set on the enjoyment of popular music. The world of music has a galaxy of stars whose records are collected, and the music forms a constant background to most activities. Almost as popular as the artists are the disc jockeys who operate over "soul stations" and converse in the language of the audience. One might assume from the dress, the music, the dancing, and the humor that the world that these youngsters populate is tension-free. The truth of the matter is that these young blacks are trapped, and have practically no control over their environment. Though this is a true picture of their world, it does not correspond to the image they have of themselves or the impression that they try to communicate to others. These youngsters experience and manifest a certain zest in their "life style" that is far removed from self-pity. This "joy of life" element seems to come particularly to the fore when they are not in contact with the larger society. There is even a sense of superiority over whites, in that one has "soul." One has the closeness of a "soul brother or sister." One has the ability to understand and enjoy life. One has "soul."

The behavior patterns of these youngsters are now in transition. A small but ever growing number have achieved a new sense of awareness. They are aware of their position in the larger society and for the first time feel that they can exercise some control over the direction that it will take.

This awareness has taken the form of racial pride—a pride in blackness. Though it is being exploited by some blacks, it seems to have solid roots and could in time have a dramatic impact upon the entire black community. The most tangible evidence of this pride is seen in the hairstyles. It is acceptable and correct to wear an "Afro" as opposed to the traditional hairstyles of old. The dress is beginning to change, and more people are wearing African-style clothing. This behavior is not restricted just to youngsters, but has spread and gained acceptance in the older age groups as well. Nor is it restricted to the ghetto. It is honestly being practiced by many middle-class blacks.

In the past there was a tendency to escape, as it were, from one's skin, but now the trend is to the opposite pole and one finds pride in one's blackness. Speculation concerning the effect this new means of expression will have upon the behavior patterns of the hard-core youths has to be made with great caution, for few if any studies have been made. What seems to be coming through is the impression that the members of the hard core will benefit from the presence of these aware young people in their midst. These young people have a great deal of pride in themselves, and this pride will surely be reflected in their work. They seem to possess a great deal of confidence in their ability, a confidence that does not stem from insecurity but rather from a new-found sense of personal worth. These young people want meaningful jobs, but not at the price of their dignity.

The number among the hard core who make up this group is at the moment very small. They are, however, articulate and aggressive. The early identification of these youngsters in a hard-core program and the placing of them in leadership roles will greatly benefit the entire program. One cannot identify by merely seeking out the wearer of the "Afro," for many people have adopted the hairstyle, but have not yet become aware of themselves. It is far better to observe the behavior patterns of the group and seek out those who tend to take a great deal of pride in themselves and the tasks they have to perform.

In the examination and presentation of a profile of the hard core, a great deal of the emphasis has been placed on this first segment. They represent the largest and the most volatile of the six groups described earlier. This group is also growing at the fastest rate and, being the youngest, will have the longest period of time to spend in the job market.

If a company had to select a group for preferential treatment, this should be the group. The recruiting, training, and job-placement energies should be concentrated here.

MEN AND WOMEN NEGRO MIGRANTS 45 AND ABOVE

This group can be further subdivided into pre-WWII migrants and newly arrived migrants into the cities of the North and West. Most of the features attributed to one group will also be present in the other. The main difference will be that the pre-WWII group will have had some industrial experience, gained in the war plants during the second World War and the Korean conflict.

Throughout the 1900's and particularly in the past 30 years, the Negro population of the United States has been steadily moving from the rural areas of the South into the cities of the North and West. In 1910, 2.6 million Negroes lived in American cities—27 percent of the nation's Negro population of 9.8 million. Today approximately 15 million Negroes live in urban areas—roughly 68 percent of the Negro population of about 22 million. In 1910, 9 percent lived outside the South. Now, almost 10 million—close to 50 percent—live in the North and West. During this same period white migration to the United States dropped dramatically after stringent restrictions were adopted in the 1920's.

Negro migration from the South began after the Civil War. The movement accelerated during WWI, when floods and boll weevils hurt farming in the South and the new industrial demands of the War created thousands of new jobs for unskilled workers in the North. After the War, the shift to mechanized farming spurred the continuing movement out of the South.

Though the depression slowed the pace of the movement, the outbreak of WWII restored it to its accelerated pace as the expansion of industrial employment in the northern and western cities attracted thousands more.

Three major routes carrying Negroes from the South have developed. One runs along the Eastern Seaboard toward Boston, another north from Mississippi toward Chicago, and the third west from Texas and Louisiana toward California.

Negroes in the North and West are now so numerous that natural increases rather than migration provide the greater part of Negro population gains there. Though Negro migration has risen steadily, it constitutes a constantly declining proportion of Negro growth in these regions; that is, the point has been reached where the Negro population of the North and West will continue to expand significantly even though migration from the South has dropped substantially.

The Negro population in the South is itself becoming urbanized. In 1950, there were 5.4 million southern rural Negroes; by 1960, 4.8 million. But this decline has been more than offset by increases in the urban population. These figures indicate that Negro migration from the South into the North and from the farms into the cities, which has moved at an accelerating rate for the past 60 years, will continue unless economic conditions change dramatically in either the South or the North and West. This conclusion is reinforced by the fact that most southern states have also experienced outflows of whites in the past decade.

The Negro population is growing faster, both absolutely and relatively, in the larger metropolitan areas. The 12 largest central cities (New York; Chicago; Los Angeles; Philadelphia; Detroit; Baltimore; Houston; Cleveland; Washington, D.C.; St. Louis; Milwaukee; and San Francisco) now contain over two-thirds of the Negro population outside of the South, and one-third of the Negro total in the United States. In six (Chicago, Detroit, Cleveland, St. Louis, Milwaukee, and San Francisco), the proportion of Negroes has at least doubled since 1950. In 1968, seven of these cities were over 30 percent Negro, and Washington, D.C., was two-thirds Negro.

Education of the migrant. These adults are the products of the inadequate rural school systems of the South. They have lower levels of educational attainment and smaller vocabularies, and usually left school before receiving a high school diploma. The low quality of education offered in these schools, situated in the most poverty stricken section of the country, is attested to by the fact that the

twelfth-grade Negro in the nonmetropolitan South is 1.9 years behind the Negro in the metropolitan Northeast, who is 3.3 years behind his white counterpart.[6] The quality of education offered by
these southern schools is diminished further by use of curricula and
materials poorly adapted to the life experience of the students. With
respect to equipment, the Coleman Report states that "Negro pupils
have fewer of some of the facilities that seem most related to achievement. They have less access to physics, chemistry, language labs; there
are fewer books per pupil in their libraries; their textbooks are less
often in sufficient supply."[7]

Current estimates indicate that there are approximately 16.5
million educationally disadvantaged Americans (those with less than
an eighth-grade education). While the exact figures are not available,
it is likely that a disproportionate number are Negro. Census data
establish that 36.9 percent of Negroes over 25 years of age, but only
14.8 percent of whites, are functionally illiterate.

As though all the foregoing were not enough, the Negro migrant
(even pre-WWII) is faced with a rapid and accelerating change in
the technology of the industrial scene. These changes, which also en-
compass the world of automation, will place a heavy burden on the
training required of a hard-core program.

Many of the members of this group will be women and men who
serve as individual heads of households. Many, if not all, will be
recipients of some form of public assistance. Approximately 7.5 million persons are reached through some form of welfare program each
month. This figure needs to be broken down so that it can be more
meaningfully examined:

- 2.7 million are over 65, blind, or otherwise handicapped.
- 3.6 million are children whose parents do not or cannot provide financial support.
- 1.2 million are the parents of these children. Of these, over
  one-third are mothers and less than 200,000 are fathers; about
  two-thirds of the fathers are incapacitated.

---

[6] *Equality of Educational Opportunity*, U.S. Department of Health, Education, and
Welfare, Office of Education, Washington, D.C., 1966, p. 20. This report, generally re-
ferred to as the "Coleman Report," was prepared pursuant to Section 402 of the Civil
Rights Act of 1964.

[7] *Ibid.*, pp. 9–12.

Monthly payments vary widely from state to state. They range from $9.30 per recipient per month in Mississippi to a high of $62.55 per month in New York. In fiscal 1967, the total annual cost of the program, including Federal, state, and local contributions, was approximately $2.0 billion, providing an average of about $36 monthly for each person involved.

When programs are designed to bring the hard-core unemployed from this group into the workforce, attention must be paid to the problem of child care. Parents will be most reluctant to leave their children unless they have some assurance that they will be cared for properly. This, of course, introduces another cost factor into the formula. One must also address the problem of making the pay equal to or better than the present welfare receipts. Many mothers will want to work. A recent study of about 1,500 welfare mothers in New York indicated that 80 percent of all mothers would prefer to work for pay than to stay home.

Attitudes. The members of the 45-plus group, from all indications, are willing to work if given the opportunity. Unlike the young blacks, they are less likely to turn down entry-level jobs that may appear dead-end. Being primarily from the South and having grown up in an atmosphere that discourages comment or complaint, they are usually interested in a "job." The type of job or where it might lead is not the major question. Steady work at a fair salary is the end objective of this age group.

If they migrated before or during WWII, many will possess some industrial experience, and the amount of general training needed to familiarize them with schedules and procedures will be relatively minimal. If, however, they are recent migrants, they will need a great deal more help in grasping the industrial tools. It is to be expected that this age group will fit in with a white workforce with much less abrasiveness than the young black members of the hard core. They should also represent a much stabler workforce.

THE PUERTO RICAN HARD CORE

Puerto Ricans are citizens of the United States, with freedom to enter and leave the continental boundaries of the United States at any time.

According to a United Nations report, it took 200,000 years for the world's population to reach 2,500 million, but it will take less than 30 years to add another 2,000 million.[8] The United Nations report isolated the small island of Puerto Rico as an illustration of the serious problem that rapid population growth presents. The economy was dependent upon sugar and was a one-crop, export-oriented island with a small land area, a large and growing population, and a very low per capita income. Per capita income in 1947 was a mere $284 per year.[9]

During a short span of time (1945–1962), a total of 578,000 Puerto Ricans came to the mainland of the United States; this number constituted 85 percent of the total Puerto Rican emigration during the 20th century. Those people who are the worse off, with respect to others in the economy, have the greatest incentive to migrate. Thus the migrants are those with low skills and usually low educational attainments. The typical migrant is usually younger than those who remain; 85 percent of those who emigrated were in the 15–44-year-old bracket;[10] yet this group constituted just 42 percent of the Puerto Rican population.[11]

Many of the early migrants in the 1940's and 1950's were single workers who secured jobs, saved some money, and then sent for the remainder of the family. This behavior conforms to a similar pattern observed in other migrant groups who came to the United States in earlier periods. The educational level of the migrant to the United States was a median of 8.4 years for males and 8.2 for females, compared with a rate of 10.6 for the United States average. The migrants lacked any industrial experience and sought jobs in the United States

---

[8] *The Future Growth of the World Population,* United Nations, Department of Economic and Social Affairs, Population Division, Population Study No. 28, United Nations, New York, 1958, p.v.

[9] Harvey S. Perloff, *Puerto Rico's Economic Future,* University of Chicago Press, Chicago, 1950, p. 50.

[10] This percentage was obtained from the ramp survey conducted at the airport in San Juan for a sample of passengers arriving at and departing from Puerto Rico for the years 1957 to 1965. Further information can be found in a report published by the Commonwealth of Puerto Rico, Department of Labor, Bureau of Labor Statistics, *Characteristics of Passengers Who Traveled by Air Between Puerto Rico and the United States* (San Juan, Commonwealth of Puerto Rico, 1957–1963).

[11] *Census of Population: 1960, Characteristics of the Population,* Part 51–14, Vol. II, United States Department of Commerce, Bureau of the Census, United States Government Printing Office, Washington, D.C., 1963.

that required little or no skill.[12] Coupled with the very serious problem of language was the real problem of discrimination in employment.

Puerto Ricans were looked upon as being different and foreign
and suited mainly for the low-paying, dead-end types of jobs. Most
Puerto Ricans feel that they are considered outsiders. They resent the
unwritten but obvious assignment to ghetto type of dwellings from
which there is no visible escape hatch. They feel that they are exploited by neighborhood merchants who populate the area and that
they are forced to attend schools that seem unrelated to their needs.
They seem to have many of the complaints of the Negro neighborhood. Because of their job-hunting experiences, the attitude hardens
that they must accept the bottom-of-the-ladder job. They have a real
distrust of industry, and special efforts will be required to convince
them that they can share the economic pie. This will require programs designed with the aid of Spanish-speaking people who are capable of working in administrative positions.

THE MEXICAN-AMERICANS

The Mexican-American is hardly ever in the news; and, unless
one lives in the Southwest, one is hardly aware of his existence. This
general lack of information exists despite the fact that the Mexican
Americans are the third largest minority in the United States.[13] The
Mexican-American ethnic group is largely concentrated in the five
western and southwestern states of Arizona, California, Colorado,
New Mexico, and Texas. It constitutes over one-tenth of the total
population of the five states combined. The proportions range from 9
percent in Colorado and California to 28 percent in New Mexico. Of
the 3,464,999 persons who, according to the 1960 Census, constitute

---

[12] The director of employment in the Department of Migration in New York City
indicated that from his experience very few Puerto Rican migrants have the opportunity
or desire to learn new skills and upgrade their economic position. The migrants do
emphasize to their children the value of hard work in school in order to advance themselves economically. The migrants, however, are content to hold down decent jobs and
support their families. Most do not have the time to worry about job advancement,
but hope that economic success will come to their children.

[13] George E. Simpson and J. Milton Yinger, *Racial and Cultural Minorities,* Harper,
New York, 1958, p. 811.

the total population of Spanish surnames in the Southwest, 2,844,348 live in two states: California and Texas. Mexican-American communities exist in a number of other cities, such as Chicago, Detroit, Gary, and Kansas City. It is a fast-growing group, showing a 51 percent increase between 1950 and 1960, contrasted with a 39 percent increase in the total population of the five southwestern states. During this ten-year period the population of Spanish surnames increased most in California, by 88 percent contrasted with 49 percent for the total population.

Some of the Mexican-Americans are the descendants of the people who lived in these territories before they became part of the United States. The vast majority, however, came after 1900 as part of the great wave of immigration. The Mexicans were unaffected by the restrictive immigration laws of 1921 and 1924, which virtually shut off the supply of labor from southeastern and eastern Europe. They entered the American labor market as common laborers, and their employment, whether agricultural or industrial, was largely periodic and migratory.

Concentration in unskilled occupations means, of course, that Mexican-Americans characteristically earn much less than most other groups in the United States. Thus, in 1960, the median annual income of all wage and salary earners among the "white" segment of the U.S. population was slightly more than $3,000, while the comparable figure for Mexican-Americans in the Southwest was closer to $2,000; among urban males the earnings in the two groups were about $4,800 and $3,200 respectively. Income levels vary from state to state for most groups, with Mexican urban males showing in 1960 a strong contrast between a median of about $4,180 in California and about $2,300 in Texas, the two extremes.

Inspection of family incomes in the Southwest shows that more than twice as large a proportion of urban Mexican-American families (31 percent) as Anglo-American families (13 percent) earned less than $3,000 in 1960. In Texas, where they fare worst among the five southwestern states, over one-half of all Mexican-American family incomes fell below the $3,000 figure.[14] And in California, where they fare

---

[14] U.S. Bureau of the Census, *1960 Census of Population*, Persons of Spanish Surnames, Final Report PC (2)–1 B, Washington, D.C., 1963, Table 1; Characteristics of the Population, Vol. 1, Part 1, Washington, D.C., 1961, Table 10; State Volumes Tables 13 and 15.

best, and even in those counties where the Mexican-Americans have the highest incomes, the incomes were substantially lower than those of the Anglo-Americans.

Consistent with their occupational and income position, the educational attainment of Mexican-Americans also ranks substantially below that of the majority of the population. In 1960 the median number of school years completed was 8.1 for Mexican-American males (in urban areas, 8.4), as compared with 10.3 (urban, 11.0) of the total U.S. male population 14 years old and over. In the five southwestern states the median school years completed by Mexican-American males ranged from a high of 8.9 years in California to a low of 6.2 in Texas.

Although the limited assimilation and acculturation of Mexican-Americans have often been discussed by the social scientists, there are very few scholarly studies that isolate the factors responsible for this situation. A recent effort along this line is the work of Florence Kluckohn and Fred Strodtbeck,[15] who suggest that the slow rate of assimilation is attributable to sharp differences between the "deeply rooted" value orientation of the original Mexican culture and those of the dominant American culture.

They say that the two cultures approach universal human problems with opposite orientations. When the question of man's relation to nature arises, "subjugation to nature" is the view held by the Mexican culture, whereas "mastery over nature" is the American view. Thus they conclude that this note of fatalism in the attitude and behavior of Mexican-Americans springs from the belief that the environment cannot be controlled.

As for time orientation, the Mexican culture stresses the present, and the American the future. Mexican-Americans regard the future as both vague and unpredictable. Planning for the future, so much a part of American culture, is therefore not their way of life. In the appraisal of persons, the primary questions in the American scale are, "What does the individual do?" "What can he or will he accomplish?" But in the Mexican scale the primary questions are, "¿Quién es?" ("Who is he?") and "¿Qué clase de persona?" ("What kind of person?").

---

[15] Florence Kluckohn and Fred L. Strodtbeck, *Variations in Value Orientations*, Row, Peterson, Evanston, 1962.

These various circumstances have contributed to the isolation of the Mexican-American from the mainstream of life in the United States. Not mentioned but surely present and playing a dominant role in this separation is the discrimination that takes place in jobs, housing, and education. The most recent systematic study[16] on this subject found Mexican-Americans to be highly segregated from the majority population in most of the 35 cities of the Southwest that it examined. This conclusion was based on the analysis of the 1960 Census tract data by means of an index of segregation ranging from 0 to 100. (Zero would indicate no segregation, and 100 would mean complete segregation.) The index of Mexican-American segregation from Anglo-Americans ranges from a low of 30 in Sacramento, California, to a high of 76 in Odessa, Texas, with a mean of 54. If these facts are kept in mind, it is easier to understand the hard-core unemployed Mexican-American, and it is easier to understand that he brings with him the marks of present and past segregation and isolation.

The most striking feature of the Mexican-American hard core is that it is young. For the Mexican-American population as a whole, the median age is close to 20, as compared with 28.8 for the total U.S. white population. The median age for nonwhites is 21.4 years.

Whether they are first, second, or third generation, their principal language, especially in interpersonal relationships, seems to be a form of Spanish-American that is a local Spanish dialect heavily intermingled with Hispanized English terms and Anglicized Spanish words. The schools largely failed in their function of teaching English. Frequently Mexican-American young people are deficient in informal English: They do not know how to use the "small talk" so important in everyday encounters. For this reason they tend not to have encounters with Anglo-Americans.

Male children are indulged and given a great deal of freedom of movement, for which they are not expected to account to their parents. Their outside activities are considered part of the process of becoming a man. Such indulgence might hamper the development of the "need of achievement" in educational and occupational endeavors. On the other hand, girls are closely supervised and taught

---

[16] Robert Ewin and Raymond Katzell, *Tests and Fair Employment,* New York University Press, New York, 1968.

their place in the home, although there is some indication that the norms of feminine behavior may be changing in the direction of more freedom.

The theme of honor, like that of *machismo* (manliness), is predominant in the orientation the Mexican-American child receives at home. Honor in this conception is tied to an inner integrity, which every child inherits as part of his Mexican-American birthright and which he is to guard jealously against all. It manifests itself in "extreme sensitivity to insult," displayed so often by Mexican-American youths. Their reactions, consistent with their concept of honor, seen from the Anglo-American point of reference, often appear as touchiness.

In the recruitment and training of these young people this one area will be the most critical. Years of exclusion have created a reservoir of hate and distrust for the "Anglos," and any gesture that can be misinterpreted will almost surely be taken as a slight.

Tied to the value system is the emphasis placed on respectful conduct. Both boys and girls are urged to show respect, obedience, and humility in their behavior toward parents and elders and are drilled in courtesy. It is interesting that a pool of hate may exist for someone; and yet, if that person is in authority, his position is respected though he is not.

Much like delinquent behavior, lack of ambition is a stereotype widely linked in the Southwest with the image of Mexican-Americans in general and Mexican-American youths in particular. Despite these beliefs it seems clear that many Mexican-American youths, if they could fulfill their aspirations and expectations, would substantially exceed their parental generation in occupational and educational status. Since education constitutes an important means of realizing occupational ambitions, it is significant that a recent Los Angeles study shows many Mexican-American male high school seniors expecting to go on to college. Merely 5 percent of their fathers attended college, but 44 percent among them expect to do so.

It appears safe to say that there is a very sizable percentage of Mexican-American youths with values differing from and goals exceeding those of their fathers but that are quite similar to both the goals and values of the majority youth. Whether Mexican-American youths follow the pattern of upward mobility in the industrial world largely depends upon the opportunities that are open to them. The majority seem to want to participate in the American Dream, but they are not convinced that the many obstacles that have long stood in their way are not still present.

Industry faces several major problems if this group of Americans is to be brought into the mainstream. The concentration in the Southwest is the biggest problem since it may be difficult to create enough jobs soon in this section of the country to make any meaningful dent in the unemployment problem that exists within this group. The possibility of encouraging outward migration seems dim in view of the cultural ties and perhaps even more important the fear of venturing outside of familiar surroundings in search of employment. The life they live is far from satisfactory, but it is conducted in an environment that is known. The second problem, though not as difficult as the first, is to convince these young Americans that jobs are available and that these jobs have occupational ladders that they will be permitted to climb.

The fact that this group is concentrated in just five states poses the major problem. The culture is based on a strong family-centered relationship, making it difficult to encourage outward migration. Any firm doing business in the Southwest and considering the introduction of a program to utilize the Mexican hard core should understand these cultural patterns and adjust in order to accommodate them.

THE AMERICAN INDIAN

Information on the employment and training of the American Indian is sparse. It is estimated that, of the approximately 800,000 Indians living in the United States, 250,000 have left the reservations and drifted into the urban centers.

The in-migration has been taking place over the last three decades, but the small numbers cause it to pass unnoticed when one compares it with the mass movement of blacks from the South to the North and West. The Indians in a real sense are the "invisible minority" in the urban setting.

The problems faced by the city-dwelling Indians are in a sense similar to those faced by other minorities but also different. There are the usual problems: housing, lack of skill, and schooling; but, because the Indians desire to maintain their communal and social separation, the gap is widened and the alienation more severe. Life on the reservation is responsible for the creation of a passive approach to life rather than one of aggressiveness. The Indians, according to a worker in the San Jose, California, Indian Center, are innately shy and when turned down on a job application tend to accept the rejection without question. For these reasons, over a third return to the reservation after having spent less than a year in the urban centers.

Ray White, an Indian and director of the United American Indian Center in San Jose, California, said that little training is being offered the Indians to fit them for jobs: "There is a program that will bring the Indians into the city and enter them in a trade school. Usually there is a waiting list for this type of training. The problem, however, is that because of poor orientation and follow-up the Indians finish the training and return to the reservation, where there is usually no work available. The few Indians who remain in the cities are usually those who were in the service or had come off the reservations to attend school."

The Indians' main complaint, as voiced by Mr. White, was the failure of the Bureau of Indian Affairs to take a firm stand and begin to train Indians for meaningful jobs. Even more than jobs, however, the Indians want training at the college level so that trained men and women can return to the reservations to help the others.

Mr. White said that a few reservations have some Government work to do. For example, at Fort Peck, in Poplar, Montana, the Indians are repairing small weapons for the armed forces.

Because the problems of long-term unemployment among Indians —who have sometimes been called "the hardest of the hard core"— relate to philosophies of life among Indians, which are very different from the basic philosophies of life that guide Western civilization and have roots that go even deeper into American history than the nation's black roots, it is possible that constructive approaches to solving the unemployment problems may require different philosophies as well as different methods.

3. Recruiting the Hard Core, and Resource Organizations

FOR MOST PEOPLE, the search for a job is not a relatively complicated matter. Most make use of the want ad section of the daily newspaper or depend upon acquaintances who inform them of job opportunities. For the hard core the matter is not so simple. Lack of marketable skills, low educational levels, police records, and a history of rejection because of discrimination have caused members of the hard core to virtually give up any hope of obtaining meaningful jobs in the industrial sector.

They are further frustrated, when they do apply, by the seemingly complex application blanks and other forms that they are required to complete. Often it is even more subtle than this; the decor of the personnel office and the formality of the receptionist sometimes served as the reason they never entered; and, if they did, they turned off, walked out, and never returned.

Advertisements addressed specifically to the residents of the ghetto will generally fail to reach the hard core. These appeals are viewed as being directed to those residents of the black community who are educated, possess some skill, and lack a police record. If the real hard core are being sought, newspapers and magazines may prove to be the weakest recruiting vehicles. As a result, it takes imaginative effort on the part of the company to recruit the real hard core. As an example, an executive assistant dealing with the hard-core program at a life insurance company advised: "Take a card table under your arm and your own folding chair. Go into the black barber shops in the ghettos. Set up your employment office right there. Since you can't be in all the shops, enlist the barbers as your recruiters."

The Importance of Defining "Hard Core"

Since the target group that is being sought is not identified merely by skin color, it is important that recruiting directions be stated clearly so that the correct group is sought and hired. For example, when a large West Coast employer began to recruit the hard core, his quotas were filled ahead of schedule, and training began. The reports he began to receive were all favorable. None of the expected problems of lateness, absenteeism, or inability to grasp the material was reported. Workers were actually being placed on the job ahead of schedule and, except for a few personality conflicts, all seemed to be going well. There were even some workers seeking more responsibility and showing interest in areas outside their particular jobs. As to be expected, this led the company to an investigation of the why for this kind of behavior. It was soon discovered that the new trainees were anything but hard core. Most had held jobs before; some had even left jobs to seek opportunities in this particular industry and company, opportunities that had heretofore been denied to black workers.

Many black workers are underemployed and are actively seeking opportunities to move up in their present company or to switch to firms that might offer them a chance to become qualified for more meaningful occupations.

Ford Took Its Employment Office to the Ghetto

Ford Motor Company executives began a systematic examination of the reasons that people defined as hard-core unemployed could not gain employment at Ford. Several factors were highlighted as crucial during this examination, and the recruitment program was designed to take them into account.

Most important, it was discovered, was the physical hardship experienced by the long-term unemployed simply to reach the employment gate. In the Detroit area an applicant might have to travel as much as 12 to 15 miles to reach the Rouge River plant just inside Dearborn borders. Since the hard core were broke and often fearful that no job would exist at the end of the trip, such a trip on public transportation seemed formidable. Financing the trip was seen as a major venture to many unemployed.

The task of applying for a job was further complicated by what the hard core saw as a real ordeal of interviews, examinations, and scrutiny of police records.

Ford's special effort to recruit employees from within Detroit's inner city resulted from several thousand job openings in Detroit-area Ford plants and the company's desire to make a meaningful contribution to help reduce hard-core unemployment.

Recruiting at two City of Detroit employment centers (Community Action Centers) began toward the end of October 1967, shortly before Ford resumed full production after a 67-day strike against the company by the UAW. The job openings were a combination of those existing when the strike began in September and those based on an estimate of the number of employees who might not return to Ford when the strike concluded and full production resumed. Initial contact with the centers, both situated in predominately black communities, was made by a black employee of Ford. The company had asked him to establish this contact with the ghetto following the Detroit riots.

The program included two basic departures from normal Ford employment practices. For the first time, the company hired employees off plant premises. In addition, a written test—one of the normal tools used in recruiting—was suspended for all applicants.

A month before actual recruiting began, preliminary planning by the company's labor relations staff got under way. The final plan, reviewed with industrial relations managers of Ford's manufacturing and assembly divisions, included

- Arrangements with the Mayor's Committee for Human Resources Development (MCHRD) to utilize interviewing and physical-examination facilities at the Community Action Centers, one on the west side and the other on the east side. These centers were selected because they had large numbers of hard-core unemployed registered under a new program operated by the Michigan Employment Security Commission.
- Selection of 12 experienced company industrial relations representatives to be given special training for interviewing disadvantaged job applicants.

- A revised new-employee orientation program to provide at least one hour of orientation, on company time, in which emphasis would be given to the role the new employee would play in the new job and what could be expected from the company to help the new employee retain the job.
- A series of meetings with division and plant executives to explain the program and highlight the need for sharpened awareness in helping the disadvantaged succeed on the job.

A program was also developed for foremen to insure that they recognized their responsibility to assist new employees in succeeding on the job.

The principal steps in the recruiting effort were

- Company representatives or MCHRD personnel helped applicants complete application forms.
- Interviewers spent approximately half an hour with each applicant.
- A physical examination was performed at the center, at company expense, by MCHRD medical personnel.
- Applicants were offered a choice of plants with job openings.
- Hiring was done on the spot.
- A criminal record did not per se result in rejection of an applicant, but each case was considered on its individual merits.
- A minimum of processing—for example, completion of hospital-surgical-medical group insurance and other employee benefit forms—was required at plant locations.
- Rejected applicants could be referred to city social workers at the centers, who possibly could assist them in such matters as medical rehabilitation or placement in more suitable work.
- Bus tickets for the first two weeks of employment were provided to new employees who had no personal transportation but were able to find public transportation.
- New employees without financial resources could obtain pay advances of $5 weekly for the first two weeks of employment to enable them to buy meals in company cafeterias.

At the same time, the written test was discontinued at all Ford plants.

Ford did not have to overcome much of a credibility problem because it had developed a history of employing members from minority groups, although for many companies this is still a problem that besets the recruiting process.

The Ford recruiting effort was more than successful, and approximately 5,000 workers were processed and hired through the two community-based centers. The added value of doing it through the centers was that the centers assisted in identifying the eligible applicants.

One factor in the success at Ford has not received much attention in the literature on these programs. Ford's inner city program received its greatest publicity from word-of-mouth communication by those already on the payroll. The fact that Ford was coming into the inner city to recruit, and that many of the former barriers to employment were to be eliminated, spread rapidly through Detroit.

The unofficial communications network was so effective that black migrants from the rural areas of the South responded by pouring into Detroit's black community, in effect offsetting the dent the Ford program was attempting to make in the unemployment picture in black Detroit.

GENERAL ELECTRIC USED A RECRUITING TRAILER

In Waynesboro, Virginia, General Electric Company's specialty control department found it useful to dispatch a recruiting trailer into the Negro community. The trailer was staffed by a white male GE employee from the personnel office and a black engineering technician, who was able to iron out certain isolated situations, such as "heckling" or "reluctance to be the first to walk in and apply for a job."

Though this method may not utilize community-based people to assist in identifying eligible people, it does have the advantage of being mobile and is thus able to go where the people are situated in various parts of the labor market area. The trailer can be parked in busy traffic areas and, because it is conspicuous, will draw attention. Being mobile, it can establish parking patterns that will permit people to expect its arrival at certain times on certain days and thus take advantage of word-of-mouth communication about the recruitment effort.

The GE experience showed that this technique can attract the serious hard-core applicant as well as the curious and the trouble-makers. On one occasion, for example, an intoxicated applicant showed up several times during the day and became quite loud and abusive.

Although the Negro population was not large in the recruiting area, the task force on the trailer was able to recruit 11 hard-core un-employed on its first visit. Out of this number, four were actually hired; a year later, two were still on the GE payroll. The personnel staff has scheduled the trailer approach in the ghetto on a regular basis (spring and fall) and not just when employment needs are heavy, be-lieving that GE will develop increasing acceptance in the area with this method.

LOCKHEED-GEORGIA PLANNED TO USE GANG LEADERS TO RECRUIT

The use of gang leaders was a technique contemplated by Lock-heed-Georgia Company, a division of Lockheed Aircraft Corporation. These gang leaders were to be placed on the company payroll, put through a brief orientation program, and then sent into the field. This technique was not implemented because traditional recruitment sources proved successful.

One of the major problems to be faced in using this technique would be to convince recruiters that meaningful jobs do exist and that the recruits are not merely part of a company "game." Crucial to their status as leaders would be their ability to deliver something worthwhile. Recruits for the most part would be restricted to young people.

Lockheed-Georgia's concept avoided "establishment" labels for the gang leaders; for example, the usual shirt and tie would not be required attire. Nothing would destroy the leaders' credibility faster than the belief among their peers that they had copped out.

Through the use of gang leaders, it would be possible to overcome what has been identified as a major obstacle to reaching the hard-core unemployed—a lack of credibility in the hard-core community.

PACIFIC TELEPHONE RECRUITED THROUGH PRESENT WORKFORCE

Pacific Telephone and Telegraph asked its present employees to recommend the company and the program to a friend.

Hard-core unemployed generally hesitate to apply for jobs for fear that they may be rejected for the many reasons offered in the past. They also harbor the fear that they may not be able to perform at an acceptable level. These fears and the accompanying anxiety are best relieved by their talking with someone they feel they can trust and to whom they can relate. Added to this is the plus factor that the present employee serves as an example of success and takes an interest in seeing to it that the new trainee "makes it." Present employees have long served as an excellent source of new hires, and in the case of the hard core they can help close the credibility gap that exists between the company and the hard core.

The main handicap that was discovered in this approach was that it did not bring in the true hard core, but rather seemed to have its best effect in reaching the underemployed members of minority groups. One reason for this is that the regular employees did not normally associate with hard core and also that the definition of hard core was not clearly understood.

The company also found recruitment possibilities as a byproduct of a different operation. The company had hired disadvantaged youths to canvas door to door to trouble-shoot problems in the black community. They would ask if the resident had a phone and if so whether he had any complaints or questions. These questions generally led to other questions about the phone company and eventually to the question of jobs. Though the initial purpose of the survey was not recruitment, these young people passed on leads to the recruiting officer. Many leads led to the employment of minority group members.

In an earlier effort, after joining "Plans for Progress," the company found that it had to take considerable initiative to reach minority groups. The most effective recruiting method, the company discovered, was to appoint minority recruiters, blacks and Spanish-speaking people, "who became walking employment offices in stores, drugstores, barber shops, beauty parlors, pool halls, anywhere the minority communities congregated."[1]

---

[1] *Putting the Hard-Core Unemployed into Jobs,* Part II, Case Studies, National Citizens Committee for Community Relations and the Community Relations Service of the U.S. Department of Justice, U.S. Government Printing Office, Washington, D.C., 1967.

AVCO RECRUITED THROUGH ESTABLISHED AGENCIES

Following the method most companies choose, AVCO Corporation recruited through established Government and private agencies to build a workforce in its Roxbury subsidiary. The principal agencies employed were the Urban League, the Opportunities Industrialization Center, and the Concentrated Employment Program.

The company tried newspaper ads in the beginning, but found them ineffective. In retrospect the company found that the hard core did not read or did not believe the ads because in the past such ads had usually been "loaded" with requirements that black workers could not meet.

Ultimately, the company found that the greatest boost for its recruiting program came from the hard core who had been interviewed by the company and hired for work. The company now believes that word of mouth beats any other form of recruiting.

The AVCO program made a special effort to dig deep into the difficult layers of the long-term unemployed. For example, the company went to the penal institution on Deer Island, outside of Boston, and recruited inmates who were about to be released. According to Ronald Neal, director of training for the Roxbury plant, the inmates who accepted employment turned out to be some of the best trainees. [Ford Motor Company also is experimenting with 70 released inmates in its hard-core program; but, since the program has just begun, evaluation cannot yet be made.]

At AVCO the normal job requirements were completely eliminated. The company did not negatively consider past work record, prison record, or any past job irregularities, such as a history of absenteeism or lateness, or the fact that an applicant might have held four different jobs in the past four months.

LOCKHEED-SUNNYVALE USED 33 DIFFERENT AGENCIES

Lockheed Missiles & Space Company did not attempt to use newspaper ads to reach the hard core for its Sunnyvale program. The company wrote letters to 33 different agencies, Government and private, to seek qualified trainees. One aspect of this effort that was somewhat different was Lockheed's use of the Mexican-American Opportunity Center to contact Mexican-Americans. This seems to be the primary center of contact between employers and unemployed Mexican-Americans in the San Jose area.

COCA-COLA USED AN INFORMAL APPROACH

The Coca-Cola Company used a more informal approach. After President J. Paul Austin had decided to involve the company throughout the United States in the NAB program, counseling sessions were held with all officers, department heads, and supervisors who were to be directly involved in the hard-core program. The supervisors received a thorough briefing on the methods and responsibilities of implementing the NAB program and, at a later date, were given sensitivity training.

The personnel department had the responsibility of recruiting, evaluating, and employing the hard core. Those who were recruited were obtained through three major sources—Government agencies, employee referrals, and walk-ins. Normal hiring restrictions, such as high school diplomas, clean police records, and previous job instability, were waived as much as possible. The major criterion used to select "the NAB employees" was to determine whether the prospect had the basic ability to do the job assigned.

The company feels that much of its success with the program was attributable to the personal involvement and flexibility of the individual supervisors. Formal materials were not developed. The plan was to approach this situation on a very personal, unstructured, and flexible basis.

THE USE OF TELEVISION

In Los Angeles a 19-hour "Job-a-Thon" patterned after the charity telethons was used by television station KTTV to close the communication gap between the unemployed in the ghetto and the potential employers. From Friday night to late Saturday afternoon, viewers were asked to phone in pledges of jobs for the residents of several low-income areas in the Los Angeles vicinity. The announced result was 25,000 job opportunities. On the following Monday morning more than 6,100 job seekers appeared at local state employment offices in response to the offers.[2]

There have been other successful uses of TV to recruit the hard core. It seems that they can be reached through this medium. Whether the message is believed is something else.

The Use of Radio

In addition to using Government and private agencies to recruit, and short of taking a recruiting task force into the ghetto, companies have found radio an effective device for reaching the hard core, if "soul" stations are used.

The transistor radio is a constant companion to many of the hard core, particularly the young. The "soul" stations are manned by black disc jockeys, who are popular in the ghetto communities. As well as playing music, the stations provide local news of interest to ghetto residents. The stations have credibility among the hard core and thus can help overcome one of the main recruiting obstacles that companies face. Also, radio offers the advantage that it is an inexpensive advertising medium.

According to Deutsch & Shea's *A Guide to Negro Media,* "the Negro population centers listed in the guide generally have two Negro radio stations, and most major markets have at least one. The Negro radio stations have a potential coverage of approximately 93 percent of the total Negro population."[3]

Resource Organizations

In many cities, community organizations have sprung up. These organizations range from those that are riding the crest of a volatile situation to those that are vitally interested in their neighborhoods and are attempting to serve as the catalysts for change. The latter can

---

[2] *Los Angeles Times,* August 29, 1967.
[3] *A Guide to Negro Media,* Deutsch & Shea, Inc., New York, 1968.

be of extreme help in guiding firms that seek an entry into the black community. It is impossible to list or describe the many organizations that now exist in black communities all over the country. It is also impossible to evaluate the programs conducted by these various groups. A checklist, however, might be of some value to companies seeking their services:

1. Don't respond to threats. Dismiss the person or persons who claim the power to stop or start neighborhood disturbances. Responsible organizations don't use fear as a weapon.

2. The group will have local residents in decision-making positions. Avoid the lone operator.

3. Respected and usually well-known blacks will have some affiliation with the organization.

4. Objectives or a statement of mission will surely be spelled out.

5. Don't shun the organization that lacks the formal trimmings. Many of these groups are inexperienced and young.

6. If you can identify a community organization that has the support and respect of the community, by all means work through that organization. If no organization exists, it is better to go alone rather than not go at all.

THE OPPORTUNITIES INDUSTRIALIZATION CENTER

If one organization were to be singled out as a model, it would have to be the Opportunities Industrialization Center (OIC), founded in Philadelphia by Leon Sullivan in 1964. OIC now has more than 25 centers in communities throughout the country; these are funded by the Federal Government. The centers are situated in the black communities and include one center in San Juan, Puerto Rico.

As of April 1969, when this report was being prepared, OIC had trained 39,656 previously unemployable or underemployed people. This year alone there are approximately 22,000 people in the program.

OIC training spans 43 different vocational areas, including business machines, electronic assembly, IBM keypunch, computer maintenance, office machine repair, and aircraft assembly (West Coast).

The program at OIC is divided into two separate and distinct sections. All applicants must take the prevocational part of the program, and then they are channeled directly into a job or into the training cycle of the program. This prevocational training provides the foundation necessary for many trainees (1) to accept the idea of going to school, (2) to understand basic communicative and computational skills, and (3) to be motivated to a point where a more than reasonable certainty can be established that they will remain on a job once they have been trained and placed. After this training, the trainees are "fed" into the vocational training courses of their choice. From this action comes the name "Feeder Program." Here is where OIC differs sharply from other manpower training programs. Its flexibility and its Feeder Program are considered by many to be the two prime reasons OIC is the great success it is.

Once a potential trainee has been persuaded to enroll at OIC, he is registered and assigned to a counselor. There his interests and desires are determined and recorded. Personal problems are discussed and steps taken to help eliminate them.

The counselor becomes the trainee's closest associate at OIC. A very personal relationship is established; and, more often than not, the encouragement and assistance necessary to keep a trainee moving ahead come in private conferences between trainee and counselor. This counselor-trainee relationship follows as long as the trainee is associated with OIC. Many of those who drop out because of serious and complicated personal matters are persuaded to return through the aid and active concern shown by the counselor.

There is no "beginning" and "completion" in the Feeder classes. When a trainee is enrolled, the teacher fits him, starting him at his level of achievement. He remains there until he receives a favorable nod from the counselor-teacher team to move ahead.

Some trainees complete the Feeder Program and go directly on to jobs under on-the-job training contracts with industry. Others go into the vocational training courses. A companion part of OIC training is the Adult Armchair Education program (AAE). This program, which is OIC's deep thrust into the centers of impoverished communities, is designed to provide basic instruction and guidance in the informal setting of a friend's or neighbor's living room. It provides educational experiences for adults, which will increase their knowledge and understanding of the world around them. It also aims to reverse negative attitudes and values as it enables the acquisition of new skills. Specific objectives of the program are to

1. Motivate people who are not receptive to formalized learning situations to re-enter a variety of adult education programs.
2. Motivate AAE trainees to begin job training programs designed to develop skills needed in the employment market.
3. Prepare trainees faced with immediate financial problems to enter direct job situations.
4. Increase trainee awareness and involvement in constructive solutions to neighborhood problems through direct participation in a range of specific and self-determined community projects.
5. Extend counseling and referral services to people on a local neighborhood basis.
6. Channel the leadership potential that is discovered in trainees into constructive outlets and develop this leadership so that it can actively be applied to help the community.

The target population of AAE is the unemployed and underemployed citizen living in poverty sections widely scattered throughout the city. The success and effectiveness of any program depend heavily upon the number of qualified people available.

In many instances attracting the talent is difficult because of the many opportunities that are now becoming available to trained or trainable nonwhite managers. Because of a shortage many programs suffer. This shortage of talent is reflected not only in community organizations but also in many of the Government-sponsored programs that deal with the problems of the unemployed. In fairness, one must not expect the same sophistication and know-how possessed by most OIC operations to exist in many programs similar in nature. Perhaps after a shakedown period and an opportunity to learn, many of these community organizations will be of service to the firm seeking to enter the black community with a program. It seems pretty clear that the organizations are going to be part of the black community for a long time. They will be dealing not only with employment problems but also with the problems of housing, schools, police, and whatever they can fit under the umbrella of community concern.

THE NATIONAL ALLIANCE OF BUSINESSMEN

The National Alliance of Businessmen (NAB) is a cooperative Government-business program to find jobs in the private sector of the economy for the hard-core unemployed. Created in the President's Manpower Message to Congress in January 1968, NAB was launched on the principle of "hire first, follow with on-the-job training and remedial counseling."

The initial NAB goal was to have 500,000 men and women on the job by June 30, 1971, in the nation's 50 largest cities. However, at the request of President Nixon, the program has been expanded to the largest 125 metropolitan areas, and the 1971 target has now been increased to placing 614,000 hard core into productive jobs. NAB has the additional task of finding productive jobs for needy youths during the summer vacation period.

The Alliance initiated its plan in 50 of the nation's largest metropolitan areas. In each of these cities a team was established, headed by a metropolitan chairman and composed of local businessmen on loan from their respective companies and a representative from the Department of Labor. The team asked local firms to pledge jobs, permanent and summer, for hard-core and needy youths. The team worked with local public and private organizations to identify and recruit workers. The Alliance in each city expedited the paperwork involved in securing Government funds to offset the costs of training. These funds are obtained through a Department of Labor program called Job Opportunities in the Business Sector (JOBS), which is sponsored by NAB. The JOBS program is now in its fifth phase of funding. MA-1 (Manpower Administration) in June 1967 was an experimental program in which companies were asked to bid on the training of 6,000 hard core in ten cities, but there was no guarantee of jobs after training. The MA-2 phase began in November 1967 and added the feature that companies were to retain the hard core after training and award bonuses for completion. For six-month retention there was a bonus of $3,800 per man. In January 1968 the MA-3 phase began. This broadened the program to a national scope and through NAB encouraged companies to train hard core with or without Government funds. The MA-4 phase was a continuation of MA-3, but with new funding. Recruitment of hard core under MA-4 contracts is normally done by the Concentrated Employment Program (CEP) of the Department of Labor's Manpower Administration, but all trainees regardless of source must be certified by CEP or by the State Employment Service to meet the terms of the contract. Under the terms of the MA-4 contract, companies must agree to hire employees prior to training. While on-the-job training is done by the

company with the contract, supportive services such as basic education, counseling, and preparatory job training (skill development)
may be subcontracted to public agencies, such as CEP, or private
agencies, such as the Board for Fundamental Education (BFE). Hard
core who are trained under MA-4 contracts will be paid the contractor's normal wage for the occupation for which training is being
given, provided the wage is at least $1.60 per hour, the minimum
acceptable wage for the program. The next phase, announced on
May 12, 1969, expanded the program to 125 cities and was designated
MA-5. One of the principal new features of the MA-5 program is that
it provides for the upgrading of present employees.

As of March 15, 1969, NAB reported that its program had up to
then resulted in the hiring of 145,900 hard core, of whom 58,050
had quit and 87,850 were still on the job, a retention rate of 60.2
percent. NAB also reported that the average family size of an NAB
enrollee is 3.65. Of the hard core now at work, 76 percent are male.
Further breakdowns showed that, of this total, 73 percent are black,
17 percent white, 8 percent Spanish-surnamed, 1 percent American
Indian, and 1 percent Oriental.

Some of the problems that have been encountered in the MA-4
programs are worth noting here:

1. Jobs offered often do not pay well enough to encourage the
   unemployed to abandon their welfare checks.
2. Some jobs evaporate before NAB can produce applicants for
   interview.
3. Job pledges sometimes go unfilled because transportation
   problems are prohibitive.
4. Some pledges are given that do not represent bona fide jobs.

THE URBAN LEAGUE

Many companies have found the Urban League to be important
and useful in recruiting the hard core. The League has a history of
involvement in industry and is changing its posture so that it will
gain more acceptance from the element in the black community that
constitutes much of the hard core. The League has branches in most
urban areas.

As this report is written, the Urban League is under contract to the Government to find, during the fiscal year ending June 30, 1969, at least 15,000 people to be trained for jobs. Fifty-nine percent of them must be hard core.

The League also conducts a preapprenticeship program designed to increase the ability of potential job applicants to pass the tests necessary to become apprentices. Titled the "Labor Education Advancement Program" (LEAP) and funded by the Government, the program is designed to bring more young people into the construction industry.

Though its major purpose is not to conduct training programs as such, the Urban League can provide consultation and can generally tap the resource people in the black community. For example, an employee of the League was asked by Ætna Life and Casualty Company to conduct a six-hour course in personal grooming for its female hard-core trainees. The League also provides sensitivity training sessions for managers and supervisors who request its consultation. For the hard core who have been hired the League will, at the employer's request, furnish counselors who will work with the hard core on problems that might hamper their effectiveness on the job, under a "buddy system."

WORKING THROUGH WELFARE AGENCIES

A large segment of the hard-core unemployed occupy the welfare rolls. Much has been written about the welfare system in America, and lately it has come under a great deal of criticism. Cities are overburdened with the mounting costs. In 1968 New York's welfare cost exceeded the cost of public education. Much of this can be attributed to the lure of the cities, with their unfulfilled promises of jobs and an escape from rural poverty. In order to relieve some of the pressure, the Government designed a work incentive program.

The Work Incentive Program (WIP) was authorized by the 1967 amendments to the Social Security Act. Its goal is to move men, women, and out-of-school youths 16 or older off the welfare rolls and into productive employment. Responsibility for the program has been assigned to the Secretary of Labor. It is administered by the Labor Department's Manpower Administration through its Bureau of

Work Training Programs, the agency that previously operated the Neighborhood Youth Corps and other antipoverty and manpower development programs.

The legislation authorizing the program estimates that the Labor Department, through WIP, can move about 757,000 welfare recipients into jobs, training, or work-experience programs, at a Federal cost of $841 million, by the end of fiscal year 1972. But the net cost will be much lower, as the Federal Government is expected to save an estimated $476 million in welfare payments. The net cost will be further reduced as the former welfare recipients move into jobs and become taxpayers. The Secretary of Labor has been directed to have 32,000 welfare clients in the program, at a Federal cost of $40 million, in fiscal 1968.

A variety of Federal, state, and local agencies are used by the Labor Department to deliver manpower services under WIP, including the Department of Health, Education, and Welfare (HEW) and the State Employment Service (SES) offices. Local welfare agencies refer applicants to the program, where they are oriented, interviewed, tested, and counseled for a period of two to four weeks by the local manpower agency (in many instances, the local office of the State Employment Service), which immediately places in available jobs those who are ready and able to work.

The remainder are moved into work-internship or work-experience programs, such as the Neighborhood Youth Corps or New Careers, or into on-the-job or institutional training programs authorized by the Manpower Development and Training Act of 1962. During this period, welfare clients who need it also receive basic and remedial education. General educational development programs are geared to help high school dropouts earn their equivalency degrees.

A person may be placed in a permanent job at any time that he is judged ready for employment by the local manpower agency. The first priority is to move the WIP enrollees into regular employment or on-the-job training. As an incentive, the enrollee is permitted to keep a sum equal to the amount of his welfare grant, plus $30, plus one-third of the remainder of his wages.

The second priority is to move WIP participants into instructional or work-experience training. During this period, the trainees receive their public assistance grants plus up to $30 a month as a training incentive.

Under the third priority, the Department of Labor enters into agreements with public agencies or private, nonprofit organizations for special work projects to employ those who are found unsuitable for training and those for whom jobs in the regular economy cannot be found. Their welfare grants are paid to the Department of Labor, and these funds are pooled to provide a sum of money that is used to reimburse the employers for a portion of their payroll costs. The enrollees are guaranteed that their total income while engaged in these projects must equal at least the amount of their assistance grants plus 20 percent of their wages.

The Labor Department will place enrollees in work-experience sites in either public agencies or private, nonprofit organizations. Work sites for on-the-job training will be handled primarily through private industry. Costs will be shared by the Labor Department; the Department of Health, Education, and Welfare; local sponsors; and, where private industry is involved, by the employer. The Federal contribution to WIP can be up to 80 percent of the total cost. The remaining 20 percent may be in cash or in kind. It must be arranged for, but not necessarily paid by, the local welfare agency. It may not include wages paid by the employer.

Eligible for WIP are members of households receiving Aid to Families with Dependent Children who are over the age of 16 and not in school full time. The exceptions are

1. The sick, the incapacitated, and the elderly.
2. Those who live too far away from a project to make participation practical.
3. Full-time students.
4. Persons whose continuous presence in the home is required because of the illness or incapacity of another member of the household.

A person who is referred to the program but refuses to participate without good cause may have his or her welfare payments cut off, though the family may continue to receive them. This action will be taken only after hearings by an impartial body. As of April 1, 1968, any state could enter the Work Incentive Program. Beginning July 1, 1968, the program became effective in each state except where state law prevented it from complying with Federal requirements.

All states must have entered by July 1, 1969. Day care centers will be established to look after the children of welfare mothers entered in the program.

OTHER GOVERNMENT PROGRAMS

The Federal Government has launched many programs aimed at eliminating joblessness and poverty. The Government has now made an effort to unify and concentrate all its manpower efforts under the Concentrated Employment Program (CEP) of the Manpower Administration of the Department of Labor.

The CEP in cooperation with other Federal agencies aims

- To coordinate state and Federal manpower efforts to make an impact on the total economic condition of the community or neighborhood.
- To involve local employers and labor groups in the manpower efforts of the community.
- To give full-scale, personalized help to the disadvantaged—not just to train them or help them find a job, but to stick with them until they have proved their capacity for remaining in productive employment.

Since CEP is based on local needs, there is no standard plan for all projects. Flexibility and personalized help to the individual are basic to the concept. CEP services include recruitment; job orientation, counseling, and appraisal; medical, social, and support services; personalized combinations of basic education, vocational training, and work experience; and follow-up and continued counseling after initial employment to help the hard core hold their jobs.

CEP describes itself as an approach rather than a separate program. It is involved with and cuts across many Federal manpower programs. CEP projects may incorporate training under MDTA, Neighborhood Youth Corps, Operation Mainstream, and New Careers, all in one package under one contract. In addition, CEP provides manpower services for Model Cities and JOBS and cooperates closely with state employment services.

Some of the milestones achieved in the Government programs,

as revealed in the Manpower Report of the President, January 1969, are (1) the Job Corps has trained 194,200 people since its inception in 1965, (2) MDTA contracts have helped train 1,034,000 people since its inception in 1962, and (3) the Neighborhood Youth Corps has trained 1,845,000 people since its inception in 1965. [The Job Corps was scaled down, modified, and integrated into the Labor Department's comprehensive manpower program on July 1, 1969, and training emphasis was shifted from conservation work to industrial occupations.]

EXHIBIT 4. *Recruiting Trailer Used by General Electric as a Field Employment Office in Waynesboro, Virginia*

EXHIBIT 5. *Instructions Given to Job Applicants at a Manufacturing Company's Ghetto Subsidiary*

GHETTO COMPANY, INC.*
A Subsidiary of Medium Size Manufacturing Company

If you are interested in joining Ghetto Company, Inc. here's how it works.

First, you register at O.I.C. at 1234 Ghetto Street, and enroll in the regular O.I.C. program.

During your first week at O.I.C. you see your counselor about joining the Ghetto Company orientation center and file an application with him. Do not apply directly at Ghetto Company.

If you are accepted, he will let you know when to report. In the meantime, keep right on at O.I.C. because you have to be keeping up your O.I.C. work to get into Ghetto Company. During this time you will be asked to take a physical examination with a local doctor.

* * * * *

When you once start at Ghetto Company here's what happens. The first day you will sign papers to put you on the payroll. Your pay is $2.00 an hour. You work 8 hours a day. If you work every day all week, you will get 40 hours of pay, $80.00 less taxes and Social Security.

The job is a real manufacturing job. You will operate machines that assemble and package materials. You will be taught the job, so that you don't need any experience beforehand. You learn to run several production machines, taking turns with others, and you take your own turn cleaning up.

* * * * *

It is also important you keep your studies going as well as learning the new job. If you have not completed your O.I.C. courses, we will arrange for you to go to classes during your working hours, for which you will be paid. At some point you will be expected to transfer to the 3 to

---

* "Ghetto Company" is a fictitious name used because the company has declined identification.

Exhibit 5 (concluded)

11:30 p.m. shift because many production jobs start you
on a 2nd shift.

* * * * *

At frequent intervals, your Ghetto Company supervisor will
talk to you about your progress, and at some point will let
you know about how much longer he thinks it will take you
to complete your job experience. It takes some people
longer than others, but about 3 to 6 months is the usual.
To "complete" your Ghetto Company job means establishing
a good work record.
   — good attendance,
   — good quantity and quality work,
   — good housekeeping and safety practices.
When you have completed your assignment satisfactorily, you
will be offered a job opportunity at other companies, including the headquarters company. If there should be no
offers at just that time, you will remain working at Ghetto
Company until there is such an offer, or you take a job
elsewhere.

* * * * *

Now here are some other points:
   — Work starts at 7:00 a.m., and ends at 3:30 p.m., with
     a half hour for lunch.
   — You have to be 18 years of age or older.
   — You will be paid for Ghetto Company holidays.
   — If you are absent for any other reason, you will not be
     paid.
   — Whenever you work on the 2nd shift, 3:00 to 11:30 p.m.,
     you get 20¢ more each hour, or $88.00 a week, if you
     work all week.
   — If your work is not turning out satisfactorily, your
     supervisor will tell you so and help you improve. If
     it continues unsatisfactory, it may be that you should
     not try to be a Machine Operator, and you will be asked
     to talk with your O.I.C. counselor about trying some
     other kind of work.
To sum it up: Ghetto Company gives you a chance to learn
how to run a production assembly machine. But more important, it gives you a chance to learn what is expected of
you in a manufacturing plant. If you establish a good work
record, you will be ready for a regular job.

4. Testing and Hiring Hard Core

THE HIRING of most semiskilled and skilled workers fits into a standard pattern for many firms: the filling out of the application blank; the interview, where job requirements are discussed; the tests that are administered; and eventually the reference checks that lead to the hiring or the rejection of an applicant.

With the hard-core unemployed it is different. "Throw the hiring manual out the window," stated Lawrence Washington, of the Ford Motor Company.

CREATING A RECEPTIVE ATMOSPHERE

The many everyday things that constitute a normal background for the ordinary worker can be subtle symbols of rejection to the hard-core applicant. The personnel departments of many companies are housed in particularly attractive work areas. The floors may be carpeted; the walls wood-paneled, decorated with pictures; and the interviewing rooms tastefully furnished and occupied by well-dressed men and women. Altogether, the department reflects the desired image of a successful, forward-looking, prosperous company —just the kind of picture to make most prospective employees eager to work there.

But the disadvantaged youngster or adult applying for a job may find the atmosphere completely foreign; it may even be paralyzing. Many hard-core applicants may be particularly ill at ease in such surroundings. They may not be able to enter such a room easily; if they do, their normal anxieties may be magnified.

For the company that has not gone to the ghetto to recruit, it may take extra effort to make the prospect of employment interviews not

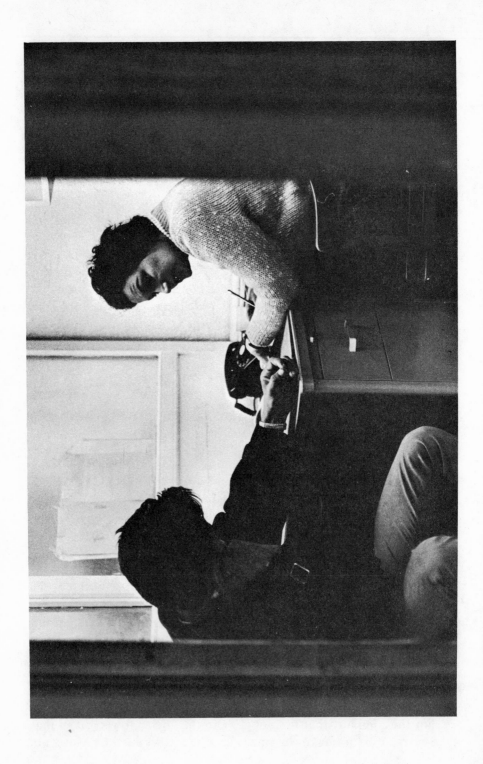

overly alarming to the hard core. This effort can start in the personnel office. The people staffing this office can adjust their normal techniques to accommodate the new type of recruit. Such standard procedures and requirements as tests, police checks, references, and a history of prior employment may have to be dropped.

A large company in the Midwest even found it necessary to examine each one of its employees on the personnel staff to determine whether they should be screened out of the hard-core recruiting program. The feeling at this company was that some employees, intentionally or otherwise, might bring to the interview portion of the process attitudes that would be abrasive in nature.

Many companies have made it a practice to hire a black person and assign him or her to the personnel office. The motive is often twofold. A minority person entering the office and spotting a black face might feel a bit more at ease and also might believe that employment possibilities exist at this particular company. The people working in the personnel office can through conversation learn and be prepared to deal with some of the questions and problems that might arise. If a company wishes to make a clear statement of its policy, black or Spanish-speaking people should not be hired merely to handle the "special" problem, but rather to participate as full-fledged members of the personnel function.

The Wall Street Journal reported that General Electric's Hotpoint unit in Chicago paid particular attention to the personnel office atmosphere. "One of its seemingly trivial but perhaps symbolic initial moves was to take down pictures hanging on employment office walls that showed only white workers and replace them with new shots depicting both Negroes and whites."[1]

APPLICATION FORMS

Many of the hard core may find the application blank a puzzle. Much of the information sought may not be known to an applicant or may not be in his possession and may be confusing. This includes Social Security number, date of last employment, and questions such as education, previous occupation, and salary on the last job.

---

[1] *The Wall Street Journal,* May 21, 1968.

For these reasons The Coca-Cola Company did not simplify its application form, but personnel supervisors did not require the hard-core applicants to complete it all on their own. Applicants were helped with the questions that were too difficult.

It is essential in almost all instances to secure information about previous arrest records. EG&G Roxbury, Inc., an EG&G Company subsidiary situated in a predominantly black community in Boston, exercised extreme care in the solicitation of this information so that applicants would not be embarrassed. Its concern was to eliminate persons who might be the source of future trouble, but not to eliminate those who had minor arrest records or arrest records that did not result in convictions.

In companies engaged in classified work for the Government, some of these application form problems can be magnified. If an applicant must pass security checks, much information may be mandatory. Some contractors have found the Department of Defense to be a source of much tension in this respect. As one company stated, "On one hand DOD is an agent for equal opportunity through the pressure of its spending. On the other hand it can be mighty tough to find minority workers who will pass security requirements of DOD programs."

INTERVIEWING

Interviews are normally held to exchange information. The applicant seeks more details about the job and the company, while the interviewer is seeking some nonquantifiable way of measuring the applicant and determining how he or she might fit into the company.

Ryerson Steel, in Chicago, eliminates all the interviewing except that which is absolutely necessary. The interview takes the form of an information session rather than the usual sizing-up period. The person who would normally interview now has the task of explaining the job and the program, the pay schedule, and other details that new employees need or have a desire to know. It is not the interviewer's job to make the selection or rejection decision; this is made by the director of the hard-core program. When applicants are rejected, the rejection is based on such information as conviction for serious crimes or evidence that a real willingness to work is lacking.

Not many companies are willing to interview as the Ford team did. They merely asked the person if he wanted to work and, if the answer was affirmative, they told him that he had a job. The average interview lasted for 15 or 20 minutes, as the company wanted to find out as much as possible about the applicant.

Thomas White, vice president of industrial relations and personnel for Bristol-Myers, stated that it is helpful if the interviewing situation is kept in a low key.

Though black or Mexican-American applicants might respond better to members of their own ethnic groups, whites can and have been very successful as interviewers of the hard core. Members of minority groups, however, tend to be very sensitive to any mannerisms or remarks that might be considered antagonistic, sarcastic, or condescending. It is not as easy as avoiding the use of the word "boy" when addressing an adult or telling "colored jokes" or keeping the interview on a friendly yet formal, last-name basis. Most whites, though not all, have developed a sophistication beyond these kinds of stumbling blocks, but are still indulging in a more subtle and insulting kind of behavior. The behavior is often normal for them and not considered insulting by the performer. In general, this behavior could be characterized as overzealous fawning, talking about all other blacks as if they were universally bright and warmhearted, or leaning over backward to prove sincerity. For this reason many firms, such as General Foods, Lockheed at Sunnyvale, Michigan Bell, set up formal awareness sessions for their personnel. These sessions take many forms, from the sensitivity-training concept to formal classroom instruction.

Robert Earle, vice president, publishing and printing of Economic Systems Corporation, Roxbury Division, made this point: "You not only have to bring the employment office to the ghetto, you have to make sure that the people working behind the desk understand something about that hard-core person. Nothing will turn a hard-core person off quicker than an indifferent interviewer or one who leans too far in an attempt to be friendly. This friendly Joe is perhaps doing harm, and doing it in an unconscious manner. He means well, he is concerned, but he has no idea or understanding of the hard core."

The Economic Systems Corporation was fortunate in that its operation was built up from the ground, so that the interviewers could be hired from among the ethnic group that was going to staff the plant.

A word of warning, however, is necessary here. The fact that a company may hire a black person to do the interviewing is not a guarantee that communication will take place. In conducting the AMA survey for this research study, in interviews I conducted among the hard core, I made the bad mistake of slipping into the language of the corner. The very first time I did this I was instantly rebuffed. The hard-core respondent did not expect this to come from me and felt forced to take up his defenses.

After settling him down I probed to find out why he took offense. His reason was perfectly sound; he knew I was going to write a research report and expected me to have eliminated the slang of the corner. He felt that by using slang I was merely attempting to appear to be one of the boys and that my reason for doing this was to open him up and get him to talk. I tried to assure him that this was not the case and that slang was used in my circle with my friends. I don't think he really believed me although we did part on friendly terms. The lesson I learned can be of importance to companies as well. Don't do things because you think they are expected. Try to be natural in dealing with the hard core. Even honest attempts might be misunderstood and act as a barrier. Don't feel that the hiring of a black face will solve all your interview problems.

TESTING

In designing a program for the hard core, the company must determine the capabilities of the trainees. In most companies this had led to some form of testing. There is little argument with the idea that testing is a valuable selection instrument that, when properly used, can provide an employer with objective information on the abilities of job applicants. This will increase the likelihood that those selected will perform effectively. Tests can also benefit the prospective employees by determining training needs and guiding them into the right jobs in tune with their abilities and interests. Xerox, for example, gives standard entry-level tests even to hard-core applicants. Those who fail are eligible for special instruction in reading, arithmetic, and basic work skills so that they can successfully perform entry-level jobs.

The Xerox experience was confirmed by that of a large department store. This company, which like most in its field is continually faced with the problem of finding competent sales people, took 16 youths from the ghetto—all of whom had flunked standard employment tests—and put them through a special ten-week training course. After completing the program, 14 became permanent employees of the department store, and 2 were employed elsewhere—even though all of them had been discarded as "unemployable" by the employers whose tests they had failed. As a group, the trainees averaged well above the sales level expected of new employees, and the individual performances of all but two of them exceeded the predictions of the sales aptitude tests.

"The time has come," a staff member in the industrial relations department of a large steel company stated, "to remedy the all-too-common practice of taking a convenient, brief intelligence test off the shelf and using it for all jobs, without considering the background of the applicant, without criteria on data relationships, and in fact without any relevance to the selection problem at hand."

The question of cultural bias has also been introduced into the testing question. A two-year study conducted by the Research Center for Industrial Behavior at New York University came to the conclusion that "tests valid for one ethnic group are not necessarily valid for other ethnic groups. That is, test scores may predict job performance for one ethnic group but not for others. For this reason, a test should not be used for ethnic groups for which it has little correlation with job performance, as superior workers stand no better chance of being selected than do poorer workers. . . ."

The question of cultural influence on test scores is not merely the outgrowth of recent concern over civil rights. Many years ago, the General Electric Company, at its Schenectady plants, found that applicants from Polish- and Italian-speaking homes were handicapped in taking verbal tests of mental ability for jobs that did not require verbal proficiency. The company's personnel men compensated for this by substituting nonverbal tests in cases where applicants fared poorly on the standard tests.

In the auto industry, General Motors, Ford, and Chrysler have now eliminated tests entirely from their selection procedures for unskilled workers. Many companies are continuing to test, but it is evident that test scores are no longer an important factor in rejecting people for employment at entry levels. *Business Week* reported that a study of "600 companies that are employing workers in ten relatively low-level specialties . . ." has produced the tentative conclusion that "the employer who drops traditional hiring standards in response to patriotic appeals may be doing himself a favor . . . that the keys to successful job performance are apt to be such qualities as manual dexterity and appropriate temperament—disregarded by many employers."[2]

One very useful insight with regard to testing was reported by Dr. Samuel Cleff, of Honeywell Corporation. Cleff has been "conducting an experiment that seeks to match unemployed people and jobs more effectively by computer." His method is to identify and categorize "positive qualities that are revealed in the total life experiences of these people," and to match these against "newly evaluated and restated job requirements."

As one phase of this project, 150 long-term unemployed people were asked questions that, in general, were designed to probe:

- "What kinds of things have you done?"
- "What are you interested in?"
- "What kinds of things do you do better than other things?"

Dr. Cleff worked closely with interviewers to insure that the questions did not have moral implications and would be answered frankly. All kinds of activities were included. For example, "a person who says he is good at shooting craps, playing pool, or gambling is skillful at activities involving probabilities. He could become a good mathematician with proper education."

Then people in 57 kinds of jobs were interviewed. The approach was, "Tell us what you do from the first thing Monday morning to the last thing Friday afternoon."

The activities described by the jobholders, and the activities described by the unemployed, were then divided into three main groups:

1. "Activities having to do with people."
2. "Activities having to do with ideas or symbols."
3. "Activities having to do with things."

---

[2] *Business Week*, February 17, 1968.

Under these classifications, Dr. Cleff came up with 16 subcategories for people and 20 for jobs. He found that "by far the greatest number of job activities fell into the third category, 'things.' Also, the greatest amount (70 percent) of activities of the unemployed had to do with 'things.'

"But most job testing today is directed toward identifying qualities having to do with 'ideas' or 'symbols,' " Dr. Cleff pointed out. These are the qualities needed for clerical, intellectual, or creative work. Said Dr. Cleff: "There are today almost no valid psychological tests to predict competence in the categories of dealing with 'things.'

"On the other hand, many unemployed indicated that they did things well involving artistic or creative activity, and had looked for this kind of job. But the job 'interviews' showed almost no need of such activity." Dr. Cleff believes that this is a major weakness in the present job system because many people's talents are wasted.[3]

Companies involved in the employment of the hard core, having faced the problems of testing, offer some hints that may be helpful to others:

1. Know specifically what equipment or tools the employee will be required to use, the level of arithmetic he must know, the type of writing he will have to do, the kind of instructions he will have to understand, and the types of problems he will face.
2. Make sure the tests are valid for the job and relate to the applicant's ability to learn the desired function. The tests should attempt to measure ability to *learn* a job not to *do* the job without training.
3. The screening, interviewing, and testing of hard-core applicants should be conducted if at all possible by personnel knowledgeable in intergroup relations.
4. Make sure tests are not screening out those applicants (particularly minority group members) who are capable of performing effectively on the job but whose cultural or economic backgrounds handicap them in taking the tests.

---

[3] *Putting the Hard-Core Unemployed into Jobs,* Part II, Case Studies, National Citizens Committee for Community Relations and the Community Relations Service of the U.S. Department of Justice, U.S. Government Printing Office, Washington, D.C., 1967, pp. 98–99.

5. Use testing as only one indicator among others in the hiring decision.

6. Remember that motivation may be even more important than test scores in indicating successful job performance.

EXHIBIT 6. *Employment Application Form Used by a Manufacturing Company's Ghetto Subsidiary*

APPLICATION FOR EMPLOYMENT   DATE:

| MISS MRS. MR. | LAST NAME | FIRST | INITIAL | (MAIDEN NAME) | SOCIAL SECURITY NUMBER |

PRESENT ADDRESS   STREET   CITY   STATE   ZIP CODE   AREA CODE - HOME TELEPHONE

PREVIOUS ADDRESS   STREET   CITY   STATE   ARE YOU A U.S. CITIZEN? ☐ YES ☐ NO

MARITAL STATUS ☐ SINGLE ☐ DIVORCED ☐ MARRIED ☐ SEPARATED ☐ WIDOWED   HEIGHT FT. INCHES   WEIGHT   NUMBER OF CHILDREN   AGES OF CHILDREN

IN CASE OF EMERGENCY NOTIFY: NAME   ADDRESS   RELATIONSHIP   PHONE NO.

EDUCATION

CIRCLE HIGHEST GRADE **COMPLETED**   GRADE SCHOOL 1 2 3 4 5 6 7 8   HIGH SCHOOL 9 10 11 12   COLLEGE 1 2 3 4   GRADUATE SCHOOL 1 2 3 4

	DATES	NAME	LOCATION	COURSE OR MAJOR	YEAR GRADUATED	DEGREE
HIGH SCHOOL	FROM / TO					
COLLEGE	FROM / TO					
GRADUATE SCHOOL OR OTHER	FROM / TO					

WHAT MACHINES CAN YOU OPERATE?

OTHER TRAINING, SKILLS OR HOBBIES

MILITARY

BRANCH OF SERVICE   FROM MO. YR. TO MO. YR.   HIGHEST RANK HELD   TYPE OF RELEASE   DRAFT CLASSIFICATION

RESERVE OBLIGATION ☐ YES ☐ NO   IF YES; SPECIFY   ☐ NATIONAL GUARD ☐ ACTIVE RESERVE ☐ STANDBY RESERVE   EXPIRATION DATE:

SPECIAL SCHOOLS OR TRAINING

PLEASE LIST MOST RECENT EMPLOYER

DATES	NAME & ADDRESS — EMPLOYER	1. JOB TITLE 2. DEPARTMENT 3. SUPERVISOR	MAJOR DUTIES	WAGES	REASON FOR LEAVING
FROM		1.		START $ per	
TO		2.		FINAL $ per	
		3.			

APPLICANT'S SIGNATURE _____   DATE _____

EXHIBIT 7. *Revised Employment Application Form, Front and Back, Reduced in Length and Simplified for the Program at AVCO's Roxbury Subsidiary, Economic Systems Corporation*

APPLICATION FOR EMPLOYMENT
ECONOMIC SYSTEMS CORPORATION
ROXBURY DIVISION
716 Columbus Ave., Boston, Mass. 02120/Tel: (617) 427-0190

GENERAL INFORMATION					
NAME (LAST) (FIRST) (MIDDLE)			SOCIAL SECURITY NO.		DATE
MAIDEN NAME IF MARRIED			IN CASE OF EMERGENCY NOTIFY: NAME TELEPHONE NO.		
ADDRESS STREET CITY STATE			NO. OF YEARS	HOME TELEPHONE NO.	
PREVIOUS ADDRESS: STREET CITY STATE			NO. OF YEARS	MARITAL STATUS	NO. OF DEPENDENTS
MILITARY SERVICE (BRANCH)		LENGTH OF SERVICE	DATE AND TYPE OF DISCHARGE	PRESENT MILITARY OBLIGATION	
SEX MALE ☐ FEMALE ☐	U.S. CITIZEN YES ☐ NO ☐	WHO DIRECTED YOU TO ESC?	IF EMPLOYED, WHEN COULD YOU START?		

WORK RECORD	
1. EMPLOYER _____	2. EMPLOYER _____
CITY AND STATE _____	CITY AND STATE _____
HOW LONG ON JOB _____ MO. YEAR - MO. YEAR	HOW LONG ON JOB _____ MO. YEAR - MO. YEAR
SALARY _____	SALARY _____
REASON LEFT _____	REASON LEFT _____
IF NOT EMPLOYED, WHAT IS YOUR PRESENT SOURCE OF INCOME?	AMOUNT?

EDUCATION			
HIGHEST GRADE COMPLETED	YEAR	SCHOOL ATTENDED	WHERE
ALL OTHER SCHOOLS OR TRAINING			

ARE YOU AT THE PRESENT TIME, OR HAVE YOU EVER BEEN A MEMBER OF THE COMMUNIST PARTY OR ANY OTHER GROUP AFFILIATED WITH OR SYMPATHETIC TO THE COMMUNIST PARTY OR ANY OTHER FASCIST ORGANIZATION...

HAVE YOU EVER BEEN ARRESTED FOR OTHER THAN MINOR TRAFFIC VIOLATIONS ☐ YES ☐ NO

IF YES, EXPLAIN...

HAVE YOU EVER RECEIVED WORKMAN'S COMPENSATION FOR AN INDUSTRIAL ACCIDENT ☐ YES ☐ NO

IF YES, EXPLAIN...

TO THE BEST OF MY KNOWLEDGE, THE ANSWERS TO THE QUESTIONS IN THIS APPLI-CATION ARE TRUE AND I UNDERSTAND THAT IF EMPLOYED, FALSE STATEMENTS SHALL BE CONSIDERED SUFFICIENT CAUSE FOR DISMISSAL.

I UNDERSTAND THAT I WILL BE REQUIRED TO CONFORM TO THE CORPORATION'S RULES, REGULATIONS AND INSTRUCTIONS AS MADE KNOWN AT THE TIME OF EM-PLOYMENT OR AT ANY SUBSEQUENT TIME. IT IS ALSO NECESSARY TO CONFORM TO THE CORPORATION'S REQUIREMENTS CONCERNING PHYSICAL EXAMINATIONS BY THE CORPORATION'S PHYSICIAN UPON REQUEST.

AS A CONDITION OF EMPLOYMENT IN CERTAIN CLASSES OF WORK, APPLICANT WILL BE REQUIRED TO SIGN AN AGREEMENT RELATING TO THE ASSIGNMENT OF INVEN-TIONS TO THE CORPORATION.

DATE.. SIGNED...

DO NOT WRITE BELOW   TO BE FILLED BY INTERVIEWER

INTERVIEWER	DATE	EVALUATION & REMARKS	ACTION TO BE TAKEN
1)			
2)			
3)			
4)			
5)			

EXHIBIT 8. *Procedures in the Hard-Core Program at Economic Systems Corporation, Division of AVCO; Excerpted from Curriculum Outline*

PROCEDURES

Responsibility for trainee selection will rest with the placement specialist who will also serve as processor. The total selection program will consist of the two Placement Specialists and be fortified with a physician and nurse, security personnel, testing specialists, counselor, and psychologist. Each applicant will be notified of date, time, place and person to report to for various steps in the following process: interviews, security checks, health examinations, and evaluation. The basic reason for a thorough screening process is to include applicants in the program rather than screen them out. Of necessity, persons who are found for various reasons not to be appropriate to our program must be informed that they cannot be considered at this time. In this event with the permission of the applicant, we will make referrals to other public or private agencies whom we consider to be appropriate to the problems. It may be necessary to counsel with the applicant on the advisability of seeking the kind of help he needs. The Placement Specialist must be intimately acquainted with all community resources in order to make proper referrals.

I.   FIRST INTERVIEW

Potential trainee/employees on arrival at the plant will be requested to fill out an application which will be provided. If an individual needs assistance to complete the application, Placement Specialists or other competent staff will provide help. The initial application will be more brief than our regular application. The regular form will be filled out at a later date.

On this initial visit the potential trainee/employee will also confer with a person to whom he will be assigned for the rest of the Pre-Employment Process. An attempt at rapport formation will be made at this time for the future benefits that may accrue to the trainee and the Corporation. The total program will be explained to the applying individual at this time.

II. SCREENING

There will be a security or screening check after the first conference to investigate the possibilities of police backgrounds. A police record will not be regarded as a reason for a potential employee to be eliminated from consideration; however, it would behoove the processor to be wary in considering the dangers of employing an individual who has a history of sex or molestation charges. Careful consideration should also be given to persons who have records of repeated brutality that may give evidence of a psychosis. A long history of mental illness or mental retardation may herald a poor forecast for the future. A person who is currently alcoholic or uses narcotics, barbituates or LSD is a poor risk.

III. TESTING

We have arranged with the Massachusetts Employment Service to implement the administration of the GATB. This test measures twelve specific areas. Some of these areas are overlapping, but measure different aspects of ability and personality. The twelve areas indicate levels of accomplishment and offer projections in the various areas for the potential of the trainee. Our potential trainees meet at our Roxbury plant and are transported in a group to the Massachusetts Employment Service. When they complete their testing, they are picked up and delivered to their homes by ESC processors. They are informed at this time that they will be contacted as soon as we are able to make a determination. This determination is only possible when we have received the results of the GATB, security check, and a medical examination. There is some delay occasionally in receiving certain items of information from medical laboratories or from Massachusetts Employment Service.

IV. JOINT STAFF COUNSELING

If the security check indicates that the trainee should be offered further consideration, a second conference should be arranged forthwith.

In addition to the data gathered during the first conference, there is a need to gather social data pertinent to an appraisal of the potential employee. A history of current and past participation in social welfare programs and past or present jobs may add to an estimate of his attitudes and aspirations. These factors will be valuable for vocational guidance and counseling.

V. PRE-EMPLOYMENT PHYSICAL AND X-RAY

Notification of a subsequent pre-employment physical examination and X-ray will be given, if after a security check is made, the applicant is still under consideration. If not, the applicant will be notified that he cannot be considered at this time.

Exhibit 8 (concluded)

VI. INDIVIDUAL COUNSELING

The primary purpose for these counseling sessions will be to explain in depth
the benefits to and responsibilities of the trainee.

VII. PLACEMENT INTERVIEW

The third conference will be a searching-in-depth situation. Personality should
be plumbed in as much depth as possible. Attitudes should be examined for kind
and endurance and an estimate made of potential for change if change is indicated
or desired. It is during this conference that decisions for participation will
be made. If the processor is still doubtful and is not prepared to make a final
decision one or more additional conferences may be necessary. An alternative
course would be to request the supervising counselor or psychologist to assist
in more personality research and in final decision making.

When the steps necessary for final decisions are completed, a diagnosis of data
will be made, and the decision of participation or non-participation for the
program will be made.

VIII. INITIAL PLACEMENT

Based on data collected through the pre-employment process, the trainee/employee
will be given initial assignment.

IX. TRAINING SCHEDULE

Each trainee will be presented with a thirty (30) day orientation schedule that
will include reporting time, room assignment, instructor, and counselor.

X. COMMENCE TRAINING

January 15, 1968 at 9:00 A.M.

EXHIBIT 9. *The Dove Counterbalance General Intelligence Test, Designed to Eliminate Bias Factors from Traditional Forms of Intelligence Tests*

THE DOVE COUNTERBALANCE GENERAL INTELLIGENCE TEST
(A Measure of Cultural Involvement in the Poor Folks' and Soul Cultures)

[This attempt to measure intelligence levels is oriented toward the culture and knowledge of Negro slum residents. Published by *Jet* magazine in February 1967 as the "Chitling Test," the test was revised in February 1969 by its author, Adrian Dove. It is reproduced here by permission of Adrian Dove and *Jet* magazine. The test was written, as much as possible, in the idiom of the ghetto.—Ed.]

1. "T-Bone Walker" got famous for playing what?

   (a) Trombone
   (b) Piano
   (c) "T-Flute"
   (d) Guitar
   (e) "Hambone"

2. Who did "Stagger Lee" kill (in the famous blues legend)?

   (a) His mother
   (b) Frankie
   (c) Johnny
   (d) His girl friend
   (e) Billy

3. A "Gas Head" is a person who has a

   (a) Fast-moving car
   (b) Stable of "lace"
   (c) "Process"
   (d) Habit of stealing cars
   (e) Long jail record for arson

4. If a man is called a "Blood," then he is a

   (a) Fighter
   (b) Mexican-American
   (c) Negro
   (d) Hungry hemophile
   (e) Warlock

5. If you throw the dice and "7" is showing on the top, what is facing down?

   (a) "Seven"
   (b) "Snake Eyes"
   (c) "Boxcars"
   (d) "Little Joes"
   (e) "Eleven"

6. Jazz pianist Ahmad Jamal took an Arabic name after becoming really famous. Previously he had some fame with what he called his "slave name." What was his previous name?

   (a) Willie Lee Jackson
   (b) LeRoi Jones
   (c) Wilbur McDougal
   (d) Fritz Jones
   (e) Andy Johnson

7. In "C.C. Rider," what does "C.C." stand for?

   (a) Civil Service
   (b) Church Council

Exhibit 9 (continued)

(c) Country Circuit, preacher or old-time Rambler

(d) Country Club

(e) "Creatin' Charlie" (the box-car gunsel)

8. Cheap chitlings (not the kind you purchase at a frozen-food counter) will taste rubbery unless they are cooked long enough. How soon can you quit cooking them to eat and enjoy them?

(a) 45 minutes

(b) 2 hours

(c) 24 hours

(d) A week (on a low flame)

(e) An hour

9. "Down home" (the South) today, for the average "Soul Brother" who is picking cotton (in season) from sunup until sundown, what is the average earning (take home) for one full day?

(a) $0.75

(b) $1.65

(c) $3.50

(d) $5.00

(e) $12.00

10. If a judge finds you guilty of "holding weed" (in California), what's the most he can give you?

(a) Indeterminate (life)

(b) A nickel

(c) A dime

(d) A year in County

(e) $500.00

11. "Bird" or "Yardbird" was the "jacket" that jazz lovers from coast to coast hung on

(a) Lester Young

(b) Peggy Lee

(c) Benny Goodman

(d) Charlie Parker

(e) "Birdman of Alcatraz"

12. "Here come the pigs" means

(a) Times are getting hard

(b) The candy man checked out

(c) The police are coming

(d) Something smells funky

(e) I'll blow you away

13. Hattie Mae Johnson is on the County. She has four children and her husband is now in jail for nonsupport as he was unemployed and was not able to give her any money. Her welfare check is now $286.00 per month. Last night she went out with the biggest player in town. If she got pregnant, then nine months from now, how much more will her welfare check be?

(a) $80.00

(b) $2.00

(c) $35.00

(d) $150.00

(e) $100.00

14. "Hully Gully" came from

(a) Anacostia

(b) Fillmore

(c) Watts

(d) Harlem

(e) Motor City

Exhibit 9 (continued)

15. What is Willie Mae's last name?

    (a) Schwartz
    (b) Matsuda
    (c) Gomez
    (d) Turner
    (e) O'Flaherty

16. The opposite of square is

    (a) Round
    (b) Up
    (c) Down
    (d) Hip
    (e) Lame

17. If I was playing the dozens, I'd be talking most about

    (a) Waterbread
    (b) Your Mamma
    (c) The digit man
    (d) Wrinkles
    (e) A together set

18. A "handkerchief head" is

    (a) A cool cat
    (b) A porter
    (c) An Uncle Tom
    (d) A Murphey Man
    (e) A preacher

19. What are the "Dixie Humming-birds"?

    (a) A part of the KKK
    (b) A swamp disease
    (c) A modern Gospel group
    (d) A Mississippi, Black liberation army
    (e) Deacons

20. "Jet" is

    (a) An "East Oakland" motorcycle club
    (b) One of the gangs in West Side Story
    (c) A news and gossip magazine
    (d) A way of life for the very rich

FILL IN THE MISSING WORD OR WORDS THAT SOUND BEST

21. "Tell it like it"

    (a) Thinks I am
    (b) Baby
    (c) Try
    (d) Is
    (e) Y'all

22. You've got to get up early in the morning if you want to

    (a) Catch the worms
    (b) Be healthy, wealthy, and wise
    (c) Try to fool me tonight
    (d) Fare thee well
    (e) Be the first one on the street

23. And Jesus said, "Walk together children

    (a) Don't you get weary. There's a great camp meeting in the promised land."
    (b) For we shall overcome."
    (c) For the family that walks together talks together."
    (d) By your patience you will win your souls." (Luke 21: 19)
    (e) Mind the things that are above, not the things that are on Earth." (Col. 2:3)

Exhibit 9 (concluded)

24. The first line of the original "Negro National Anthem" goes:

    (a) We shall overcome
    (b) Lift ev'ry voice and sing . . .
    (c) We're a winner, and . . .
    (d) Lord have mercy, Lord have mercy. L-O-R-D . . .
    (e) Carry me back to old
    (f) Keep on pushin'

25. "Bo-Diddley" is

    (a) A game for children
    (b) Seditty ways
    (c) A down-home singer
    (d) The latest dance from Philly
    (e) A mojoe working

26. Which word is most out of place here?

    (a) Splib
    (b) Blood
    (c) Gray
    (d) Spook
    (e) Black

27. How much does a "short dog" cost?

    (a) $.15
    (b) $2.00
    (c) $.45
    (d) $.05
    (e) $.86 + tax

28. Across the land the saying goes: "Beep-beep, bang-bang, . . . , BLACK POWER."

    (a) Can you dig it!?
    (b) Umgawa.
    (c) I can dig it.
    (d) Delta Jabberwock.
    (e) Say it loud!

29. If a dude is up tight with a woman who gets state aid, what does he mean when he talks about "Mothers Day?"

    (a) Second Sunday in May
    (b) Third Sunday in June
    (c) First of every month
    (d) None of these
    (e) First and fifteenth of every month

30. Many people say the "Juneteenth" (June 19th) should be made a legal holiday because this was the day when

    (a) The slaves were freed in the U.S.A.
    (b) The slaves were freed in Texas
    (c) The slaves were freed in Jamaica
    (d) The slaves were freed in California
    (e) Rev. Martin Luther King was born
    (f) Booker T. Washington died

ANSWERS

1. *d.* 2. *e.* 3. *c.* 4. *c.* 5. *a.* 6. *d.* 7. *c.* 8. *c.* 9. *d.* 10. *c.* 11. *d.* 12. *c.* 13. *c.* 14. *c.* 15. *d.* 16. *d.* 17. *b.* 18. *c.* 19. *c.* 20. *c.* 21. *d.* 22. *c.* 23. *a.* 24. *b.* 25. *c.* 26. *c.* 27. *c.* 28. *b.* 29. *e.* 30. *b.*

5. Training the Hard Core, Coaching the Foremen

THE NATIONAL ALLIANCE OF BUSINESSMEN reports that "experiences of employers who have brought the hard core into their plants indicate that half or more of them are ready for immediate work assignments." However, "in order to perform their jobs properly, some hard-core employees will need work in one or more of the following areas: person-to-person communication, listening, speaking, reading, writing, simple arithmetic, treatment of customers, job-related vocabulary, job-related calculations, other basic social and job-related skills."

KINDS OF TRAINING

The many training sessions that were observed in in-plant visits for this research study confirm the NAB guidelines. There seems to be a consistent pattern of hard-core training under the following general outlines:

- *Fundamental education* to bring the trainee up to the minimum school level associated with successful job performance. This is usually sixth to eighth grade, although some programs are more ambitious. Usually, this aspect of training is conducted by an outside service organization before the trainees are brought into the plant environment.
- *Social skills,* the most important of which is attitude training, developed primarily through "sensitizing" sessions of various kinds. When this is given, it usually accompanies training in job skills. The basic purpose is to stimulate proper motivation

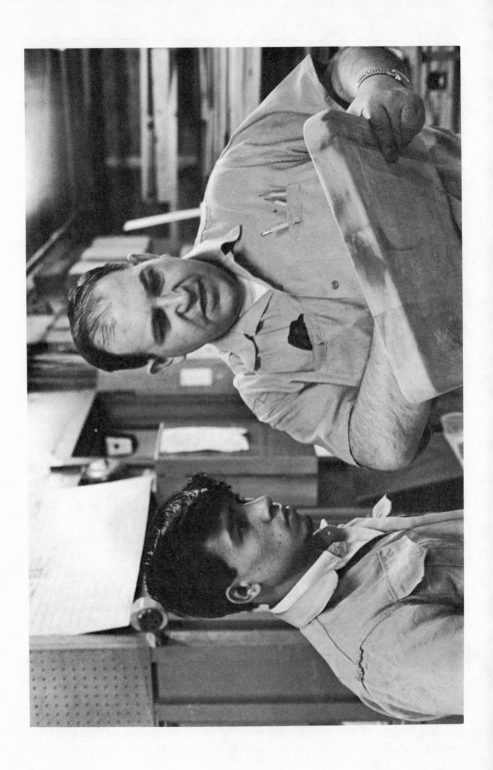

and acceptable social responses. Grooming and appearance training, when given, is usually for women workers in white-collar jobs, although some companies have made brief attempts to upgrade the appearance of male hard core; the attempts were often rebuffed.

- *Job skills development* is the heart of the training effort. This is usually given in the plant where the workers will be employed, although some companies have set up separate training facilities; others have trained hard core for whom, it developed, no openings were available, but then got jobs for the men they had trained in nearby plants requiring the same skills. Even the simplest skills must often be learned—how to load a truck, nail a board, splice a wire, make a bed.

Counseling the trainees in such matters as credit buying and budgeting may constitute a formal training program, but often it is part of the more informal supportive service offered the trainee both during the training period and in his early weeks and months on the job.

One thing that is clear in these programs is the great vogue now being enjoyed by "sensitivity training." As a result of its popularity, the concept of sensitivity training is broadening beyond its original patterns, and the phrase is taking almost generic qualities to describe everything from standard lectures to informal, fast-paced "Aha! I see the light!" sessions for both hard-core trainees and supervisors.

It is also clear that the trainees in general do not enjoy sensitivity training, attitude development, or similar sessions, but warm up rather quickly to specific training in skills for a specific job. They go along with the sensitivity sessions, and may pretend to see the light in varying degrees, but it is doubtful that such training is achieving much of the desired effect among the hard core. The main reason seems to be that the sessions seem artificial to them and fail to reach the real underlying emotions at the seat of their attitudes.

It has often been assumed that hard-core unemployed are simply unaware of what have now come to be called middle-class values. The fact is that they can quote the slogans as well as anyone: "Work hard. Save your money. Stay sober. Control your impulses. You can't get ahead without an education." And so forth. When training efforts are designed merely to restate such values in the hope that the trainees will become inspired and motivated, the programs are missing the whole point, in the minds of the trainees.

Not all companies feel that sensitivity training is required. As one supervisor stated:

> People want jobs, they want to work, pay their bills like everyone else. You hire them for that purpose, train them, and let them alone. If they want to wear "do-rags" [a kerchief worn by men who have had their hair processed] let them. What effect does it have on getting the job done? Too much time, effort, and money are spent probing, sticking, placing people under microscopes instead of letting them work. The trainees must be tired of all the studies and programs that they are forced to endure. I am sure I would be.

Another company explained that its hard-core program was a success partly because the company had used "really top-level instructors, no-nonsense guys who wouldn't let company psychologists and other intellectual types come down to have a 'dialogue' with the guinea pigs."

Training in job skills can be an elusive art if the program is not thoughtfully designed. *The Wall Street Journal* reported:

> In 1963, well before the pressure to train the unskilled had built up to its present intensity, the three [General Electric] Hotpoint plants in the Chicago area launched an experimental program aimed at fitting unemployed slum residents—mainly Negroes—into factory routine. Right from the start, there were problems, ranging from assembly line errors to a high rate of absenteeism. . . . But Hotpoint also offers some hope that such difficulties can be diminished if not entirely overcome by such measures as extensive counseling and by a more gradual introduction to full-time assembly line work.[1]

Some insight into why this was so may be drawn from an earlier article in the *Journal*.[2] For this story its author took a summer job at

---

[1] *The Wall Street Journal*, May 21, 1968.
[2] *The Wall Street Journal*, July 24, 1967.

a Ford plant, where the guide who takes visitors around regularly states, "Each worker on an assembly line has one little job to do. . . . It's simple. Anybody could learn it in two minutes."

The author of the article said, "That's bunk. Working on the line is grueling and frustrating; and, while it may be repetitive, it's not simple," and went on to recount the numerous possibilities for mistakes, no matter how well-intentioned a worker is, and pointed out "the cacophony of bells, whistles, buzzers, hammers, whining pneumatic wrenches, and clanking, rumbling machinery [that] drowns out voices."

These things were verified by an old-timer, an assembly line foreman, who said with a certain amount of satisfaction:

> These young kids ain't what they used to be. They just don't have the stuff we had in my day. We brought in these hard-core guys and trained them and put some of them to work on the line. But they found out the line is a very tough place to work. After a few hours they get so tired they're ready to drop. Every time they look up there's another piece coming at them. Every time they look up there it is, and they better get right on it.

The disorientation these things can cause can be severe to someone who has malnutrition, suspicion, and minimum self-assurance, and who has seldom in his life had to be any particular place at any particular time.

However, in designing programs to overcome this problem, one company discovered an unexpected side effect. The sensitivity training its supervisors received actually produced too much empathy in some supervisors. Once they understood something of the psychology and background of the trainees, they tended to relax performance standards too much. They began to expect less and demand less, assuming that the trainees could not perform at normal levels. In turn, as these attitudes were passed invisibly to the trainees, the trainees began to feel that they were doing an acceptable job when actually they weren't. Sloppy work, excessive scrap, delays, and errors began to be a problem. Department heads had to tell the supervisors that performance standards must improve, that the hard core don't want to be judged by a double standard, which to them may be insulting.

A frank discussion of this problem between supervisors and trainees had the effect of clearing the air and inaugurating the desired changes.

Frankness of this kind seems rare in these hard-core programs. But where men have had enough self-assurance to try it, the results in achieving communication were sometimes remarkable. One executive said:

> No matter what, we try to get everybody to talk about anything in a safe environment. Let me give you an example. [In these training programs] we capitalize on every real problem we can lay our hands on. Let's suppose you're taking a coffee break. You're out on the street. One of the guys comes along in his car. A big red light is flashing behind him. Everybody's scared in the group because it's one of our trainees. We also know he's got "stuff" in the car. Everybody's concerned about this and what's going to happen to the poor guy.
>
> But the cop clipped him just for going through the stop sign. He didn't search the car. Now the foreman—who was also the instructor in this case—got the guys together to talk about it. He asked them questions like: "Suppose he got caught on his way to the plant? Was he thinking about us when he was doing something like that? Or was he thinking only about himself? Suppose we needed this guy and we were depending on him to help us get the job done . . . ?"
>
> Let me tell you, we've gotten into the most fantastic discussions using these real-life happenings. If you want to talk about learning experiences, this is it.

But all the empathy in the world will not get a job done unless the training results in well-defined techniques and procedures each man can follow. One common conclusion companies have reached is that the training must be broken down into small, well-defined bits, from general to specific.

"When we talk," one executive commented, "we draw conclusions or make generalizations and we assume that once a person has learned a specific from a generalization he can translate the specific back into a generalization. He can't do it. This is where the problem is. *Stay specific!* Give the rule, but show how it affects the guy where he is."

This advice is corroborated by lessons learned from military training. Training in the military has been going on for a long time, and in the military the program designers had to learn a long time ago how to get a simple idea across to a recruit who might be poorly educated. One of the resulting standard formats for a military class is, "Tell them that you're going to tell them. Tell them. Then tell them you've told them."

In some of the industry training programs, instructors report that it may take two to three times longer than normal to cover a lesson with the hard core. Different ways have to be found for saying things. Every task has to be broken down into smaller, measurable units of work. And when a trainee has mastered a task, he should be encouraged. But instructors caution that rewards should be given only if deserved; otherwise the trainee—who probably knows whether he has mastered a task or a process—may very well be insulted if rewarded for substandard accomplishment. On the other hand, some hard core have not been able to achieve even scaled-down performance requirements and have been terminated. "We do fire people," an executive said, "but generally if they are trying and they are not a physical danger to themselves or somebody else, we will ride it for awhile."

It seems to be a normal experience for a company to modify its hard-core training program substantially as time goes on. Most companies are still so new to this work, however, that the basic trend of modification has not yet taken shape. One useful illustration was the experience of Equitable Life Assurance Society. When the company first hired dropouts, there was a high rate of failure.

The second year, the company worked with supervisors, picking those who were known to be sympathetic to this special effort. It was made clear that the dropouts hired would not be charged against their regular budget or their efficiency rating. They were urged to take the challenge of preparing youngsters in one year for a job in their own or other departments. There was considerably greater success. The third year, the company told supervisors to try to prepare the young dropouts for promotion and better jobs within two years, but if they could not, Central Personnel would take responsibility for them. A little better progress was made. . . . By the fourth year, it was clear that basic education was sorely needed. The company hired The Board for Fundamental Education to teach the youngsters basic reading, writing, and arithmetic (after work) so they could pass high school equivalency examinations.[3]

COACHING THE FOREMEN

It is well known that the foreman's life is one of the most high-pressured in all of industry. For example, studies have shown that foremen outnumber executives and rank-and-file employees in the percentage of heart attacks. The life of a foreman is constantly lived between the devil and the deep blue sea. And now companies are systematically making his life more difficult.

Although the general educational level of foremen is rising, industry is filled with men at this level who made their jobs the hard way, "alone and unaided," and who sometimes tend to believe that this is the only true and worthwhile way. As *Business Week* described them, they are "at the unglamorous end of the management ladder —under persistent pressure to cut costs, improve quality control, meet production schedules, and simultaneously handle sensitive workers who may just be passing through."[4]

The most popular method for coaching the foreman on his new responsibilities is to provide sensitivity training. A word of caution was expressed by one instructor, however. He said that some people who are hanging up their shingles as sensitivity trainers are not professionally qualified to lead these sessions. He cited two instances in which consultants were brought into companies to start these sessions and had to abort the projects or created a lot of bad feeling and produced no useful learning experiences. Dealing with emotions can be explosive if not well handled.

One company that decided to use sensitivity training wanted to make a special effort to design a program that was as meaningful as

---

[3] *Putting the Hard-Core Unemployed into Jobs,* Part II, Case Studies, National Citizens Committee for Community Relations and the Community Relations Service of the U.S. Department of Justice, U.S. Government Printing Office, Washington, D.C., 1967, p. 18.

[4] *Business Week,* February 1, 1969.

possible. The company brought in consultants to develop a motion picture, slides, tapes, lecture materials, and program design. These materials were to relate to the whole spectrum of relationships between the black and white races.

A large number of supervisors were selected for sensitivity training in anticipation of their assignments to take on hard-core unemployed as trainees.

The initial stages of this sensitivity training program were plagued by mistakes. The first mistake came when the program designers decided to hold compulsory Saturday sessions. The supervisors balked at this, and came close to mutiny. Saturday was their day off.

The second and more enduring mistake came when the sensitivity training planners decided that the supervisors should plunge right into the problems. The sensitivity trainers believed that this would make a big impression on the supervisors and, therefore, produce lasting results.

The session that was planned included several local black leaders who were asked to come in to present the viewpoint of the ghetto dweller. The session turned into a confrontation between the black leaders and the supervisors. The meeting ended with the supervisors feeling insulted and the black leaders feeling that they were right all along—"The whites did not really want to learn about the problem. The meeting was just another exercise that led nowhere."

It took close to six months to get the supervisors back into the spirit of the program, and even then some felt that the company was the villain for subjecting them to the insults they felt had been heaped upon them.

Despite, or perhaps because of, these incidents, the company now has what it considers an excellent awareness program for its supervisory employees. The company measures its success partly by the number of times it is asked by other companies to share both the materials and the experiences that resulted.

As has been mentioned, however, the term "sensitivity training" has come to be so broadly construed that a standard classroom lecture on the behavior norms of young blacks, accompanied by a film, followed by a discussion, now seems to qualify as a sensitivity training session.

However, a distinction must be drawn between the methods and the expected results. Sensitivity training is used because it is believed that certain results will be produced. General Motors Corporation decided to focus directly on results. As reported in *Business and Society:*

> GM's approach was to zero in not on the prospective employee but on its supervisory force. It put together a rigorous, far-reaching program to make it crystal-clear to supervisors throughout the corporation that GM meant business in this area. The program involved explaining to the supervisors what the "new workforce" consisted of—the kinds of people who had been "left out" of society—and what GM expected of its management people in this area. It was not unlike a presentation GM might get up on the market for second and third cars. As of March 12, 1969, GM had 14,794 managers participating in these "new workforce" training programs.
>
> GM takes no government money for its training programs. Asked what the "new workforce" program costs the company, the GM spokesman replied: "It's all part of the overall training program which the company conducts. Nothing unusual. Just part of the job."
>
> GM emphasized that in its approach to this problem, it decided to concentrate not on changing attitudes but on affecting *behavior*. In other words, GM doesn't see any point in trying to change the mental attitude of its supervisors. It's the behavior— the action—that it wants to lead into certain desirable directions.
>
> Asked what would happen to a supervisor whose behavior did not change, a GM executive explained, "Such a person would have to have an independent income."[5]

Certain fundamental points must be covered in coaching foremen because these points will probably apply to most hard-core training situations in which the foreman is a participant. As these were summarized by one executive:

> First, listen. The foreman has to understand that he must listen, hear the point of view the hard-core trainee is expressing. The foreman has to give him a chance to talk. He has to learn not to

---

[5] *Business and Society,* April 8, 1969.

take his anger or his inability to understand out on the trainee. The trainee may be trying like hell to communicate. This is what we tell our supervisors.

The second thing we try to get across to our supervisors is the skill of communication. This is closely related to job skill and knowledge of all the parts and processes of the work. The supervisor usually is the guy who understands the work processes right through to his bones. But what we try to do is help him learn to communicate. You might say he has to learn to convey intent—he has to convey his intent in all directions, sideways, up and down. You can't depend on the other guy's hearing it. The supervisor has to say what needs to get said, and make sure that it's heard and understood.

The third thing we try to help the supervisors understand is that with the hard core there will be a lot of testing in the beginning— the hard core will be testing them to see if they are real. Now this is a real rough thing to go through. It takes a hell of a lot out of you. You have to make it with each group separately. Of course, the more groups you make it with the better. When they learn that you are OK it makes it a bit easier. But they will have to go through this, and we tell them about it. We call this the courting, or the love-making period. It has all the earmarks of a courtship— the working out of a pecking order.

Fourth, we try to help the supervisors explore what might be their reactions to probable situations they might confront. This is similar to the way the Army trains squad leaders. Only we don't program the desired responses necessarily. But we try to lay them out so the supervisors are not caught with their pants hanging down. We try to work with them in ways they might respond not only to bum situations, but good situations as well. For example, we know they are going to run into individual acts from the hard core displaying poor motivation, ineffective performance, derogatory statements, acts of discrimination, acts of hostility and anger, negative approaches, passivity, even physical violence. We try to help the foremen make a dry run through the obstacle course.

Finally, we try to help the foreman formulate guidelines for what is going to be a total relationship between himself and the hard-core trainees assigned to him. If the hard-core guy is a Negro and he has been assigned a "buddy" he may very well have come to distrust him right off the bat as a "do-gooder," even if his buddy is also Negro. It's hard to relate to a do-gooder no matter what his color is. So, if a guy has a home problem, a money problem, a woman problem, a medical problem—and sometimes you will find a guy who has every one of these problems, plus a problem with the law, all at once together—he is worrying about these things, not his job. So the foreman has to be skillful in helping him over these problems. He must know the resources available at work if the guy needs money. The supervisor very frequently will have to dig into his own pocket to loan his trainee some money. But he'll do that only once. I know supervisors who have gone bond for a guy, who have co-signed on a car for a guy because he couldn't get credit. Now that shows a hell of a lot of faith. But you know, in each of these cases the supervisor has never been let down. What I'm saying, of course, is that we recognize, and try to help the foremen recognize, that their trainees will very likely involve them in a total relationship, and that the very center of that relationship is faith in each other.

COMPANY EXPERIENCES

In company after company interviewed for this research study, the basic problem in the training process was that the hard-core unemployed were chronically late or absent, or after a day or two they would leave, never to return.

Companies simply could not hold the hard core in these programs very easily once the trainees learned that upon completion of training they would be offered entry-level jobs at starting wages of $1.60 to $1.75 an hour. These trainees were grown men, and the wage was no inducement to continue. As one executive commented: "They seem to laugh at anything under $2.00 an hour." This problem has not yet been solved, although companies have been attacking it in various ways.

In some cases trainees are offered a "training wage" that is a compromise between welfare and normal starting wages. The trainees are given a nickel-an-hour increase after the first week and periodic increases as the training program progresses, until they reach the entry-level wage. The reason for this approach is the assumption that the trainee will think it is too long to wait until the end of the program for an increased wage, and will be better motivated by systematic increases at short intervals.

In other cases some training programs are using a sequence of badges of different colors to show recognition that the trainees are progressing satisfactorily toward completion. Counseling approaches, discussed in the next chapter, are also used. However, the problem is that in almost all companies the beginning wages are low for everyone, and the hard-core trainee is not motivated by these wages because the world in which he has grown up and lived has taught him a very different set of motivating values. It might be pointed out that the low-level entry wages are primarily a problem in holding the men in the programs. The women who are recruited for these training programs do not seem to mind as much.

Lateness and absenteeism, the worst problems, have been solved more readily. The problem results from the fact, primarily, that the plants doing the hiring are situated outside the ghetto, and the hard core lack transportation. In general, the buddy system and counseling approaches have been used to mitigate the problem—for example, a "buddy" is asked to give the trainee a lift to work or, sometimes, to go get him if the trainee hasn't shown up on time.

The Raytheon Corporation developed one of the most innovative approaches in this area. Raytheon plants are situated outside the Boston urban area, but the trainees recruited were from the Roxbury ghetto. The company furnished bus transportation from the ghetto to the training facility. The company bore the cost of the transportation service and also returned the trainees to Roxbury after their training shift. The company informed the trainees that, when they graduated from the program and became regular employees, no such accommodations would be forthcoming.[6]

At Ford Motor Company, the absenteeism and tardiness problems experienced were not attributable to transportation, but were simply

---

[6] This problem may soon be eased. *Business Week* (December 14, 1968) reported that "the Transportation Department will pay 90 percent of net costs of a new program to develop local transportation service between poverty areas and employment sites in U.S. communities. The program will be run on a grant basis by the Urban Mass Transportation Administration and will aim primarily at supporting bus operations, though it may be used to develop rail service also. To qualify, projects must be set up for at least 18 months."

a matter of lack of exposure to the industrial environment and the resulting necessity of being required to report to a given location at a specific time. This is more or less an attitudinal problem.

AVCO located its subsidiary plant, Economic Systems Corporation, in the Roxbury ghetto and set up a three-shift work schedule. Although there was no transportation problem there, the company nevertheless experienced absence and lateness on the part of its trainees. The reason was that AVCO really went after the social rejects to begin its hard-core program—ex-convicts, long-term welfare cases, and so forth. The AVCO experience finally turned in the company's favor after extensive counseling sessions with the hard core. There were other unique features of the AVCO program.

The AVCO subsidiary was started with a completely hard-core workforce. The trainers were experienced printers who were hired to set up and run the operation. The foremen were also recruited from other firms. The problems of the "old regular" versus the "new" work crews never arose.

The training was designed to provide the hard core with the technical skills needed to enter the printing trade. AVCO found that the printing trade in Boston, although restrictive, did employ several black workers who had been in the trade for years. A few had broken in during the labor shortage of WWII, and others had gotten in immediately following the War. In addition to blacks, AVCO sought qualified Mexican-American printers and finally, as a last resort, qualified whites.

Ronald Neal, director of training of the AVCO subsidiary, outlined the reasons for preference of black instructors or, as a second preference, Spanish-speaking instructors:

We feel that the black instructor is the most important element in our training package. If the instructor is black and he is training blacks, half the battle is over. If the trainee is Spanish-speaking and the instructor is also, the communication network is quickly established. I don't mean that they can both speak Spanish and hence understand each other more easily. I mean they have a sense of understanding that takes them both out of the pressure cooker. It is easier for me to talk about the black trainer and the black trainee. If the trainer is white, the trainee can find many reasons for copping out. He can claim prejudice on the part of the teacher, he can "put the teacher on" and perhaps get away with it. He can even perform at the level that the teacher expects but not really reach the level that he is capable of reaching.

If the trainer is black, most of these dodges go out of the window. The black trainer serves first of all as a model. Just standing there and performing says to the trainee it can be done by someone who happens to be black. You'd perhaps be surprised to know how little confidence some people bring through that door. The black teacher can also say things to the trainee that, coming from a white trainer, would be resented. He can pressure, push, even dress the trainee down and still be respected as the teacher.

Does this mean whites don't work? No, we have whites on our staff working every day and doing a fine job but they have to spend valuable time feeling out the trainees, not being sure what might offend and in some instances needing to dress down a trainee and finding themselves unable to do it.

(It may be noted that some companies that were interviewed complained that it is most difficult to find qualified blacks to serve as teachers.)

The training program was designed to cover five 17-week periods in which every phase of the plant's operations would be covered by the trainees. These classes were conducted while commercial work was being produced in the plant. Trainees were shown a technique and then allowed to practice until the instructor felt that they possessed enough competence to tackle, with supervision, a job that was moving through the plant. The more technical side of the trade was, of course, more difficult and required a longer training period and more supervision. Nevertheless, hard-core employees were operating expensive cameras after a relatively short period of time. They were also doing color processing and were involved in making offset plates.

Supporting the on-the-job training section of the program was a basic education module. The aim of this training was not only to provide trainees with the opportunity to acquire the needed job skills but also to improve their socialization and citizenship abilities. The curriculum, therefore, included subjects such as "The Black Man's Contribution to Early History." The course covered the era of slavery and ended with a discussion of the Social Revolution. Similar courses were held in the area of Oriental and Spanish-American history.

These dealt with migration to the United States and the social and economic problems that were faced by these groups.

The capstone to the course was a discussion of matters that dealt with the migration of whites to the United States. It was believed that, if the trainees were taught that all the other minority groups had problems in assimilating into American society and how they eventually "made it" despite their obstacles, it might give them the base for building confidence in themselves. Mr. Neal was quick to point out that the problems of blacks are not really the same as those of other minority groups and that he would be the first to admit the added burden of color. He did, however, feel that the time spent in this training was worthwhile. He stressed the value of the black, Puerto Rican, and Cuban emphasis in that it gave the members of these ethnic groups a sense of belonging. He tended to play down the comparison between migrants from European countries and blacks or Spanish-speaking people in this country.

The program also included subjects such as nutrition and diet, budgeting, safety, and first aid.

Raytheon made an effort to have a balance of black instructors as well as white in its hard-core program. Raytheon is training white as well as black hard core.

In formulating a hard-core program, Raytheon utilized its staff of professional instructors and curricula department specialists to make the effort operational. As the program continued, the company modified its training techniques and curricula when weaknesses were identified.

Raytheon's adaptation of the sensitivity training technique was used with care, in the hope of saving time, at the very beginning of the hard-core training program. The sensitivity exposure dealt with the demands of the work situation. The instructors were trying to sensitize the trainees as to what they could expect in the real work scene. Matters discussed included absenteeism, lateness, discipline, promotion, and job responsibility. The technique shook a few of the hard core out of the program in the very early stages, but those who remained showed improved records of attendance and performance while in the training program.

Another manufacturing company also set up new facilities in the Roxbury area, bringing in men from its other plants to serve as instructors. Small work groups of trainees were set up, and extra training time was allowed for teaching the operating procedures required.

At this company the foremen were brought into the training effort at its inception. The company reasoned that if the foremen and hard core had early contact it might help achieve the rapport essential to their future relationship. Many of these foremen contributed to the actual training.

At Ford the entry-level nature of the jobs for which the hard core were recruited allowed the trainees to move rather quickly onto the line and into productive jobs. Some of the hard core were productive within eight hours. Ford's on-the-job training program did not involve remedial education, but rather was designed to put men to work as quickly as possible.

Inland Steel followed the pattern of Ford, but added some academic training, enough to accomplish the jobs the hard core were trained for.

Chrysler Corporation set up "vestibule shops," adjacent to normal work areas, and moved the hard-core workers onto the line when their coaches felt they were ready. The proximity of the vestibule shops to the production lines was intended in part to allow the hard-core trainees to soak up a feeling for the work flow.

At Lockheed in Georgia the facilities for training are almost a military secret. The training facility was built quite a distance from the main plant. Lockheed reasoned that the trainee should not be identified in any way as "different" when he went to work at a regular job. As R. H. Hudson, manager of the education and training department, explained:

> The one thing we attempt to avoid is the labeling of the hard core. Once labeled, they are subjected to two kinds of treatment. Foremen and fellow workers may reject the hard core or look on him as if he were some kind of freak or, what is just as bad, they tend to be oversympathetic. The attitude of rejection is one that none of us wants and the overly sympathetic foreman or fellow worker does more harm than good. Feeling sorry for someone leads to making excuses for his behavior or permitting less than acceptable work standards to exist. Our trainees enter plants with-

out labels because their foremen have no idea where they were recruited, and at no time during their employment do we in any way identify them. We are large and it is very easy for us to do this. Smaller firms might have difficulty.

At Lockheed's main plant in Sunnyvale, California, an ambitious hard-core training program was launched in early 1967. Unlike many of the programs the author observed during his study, this program had operated long enough to iron out many problems and to offer lessons that may serve as a guide for others.

An interview with Stanley Hawkins, vocational training specialist for Lockheed, revealed a number of the program's highlights. These facts were updated just before this research study went to press.

To be accepted into the program, the Lockheed trainees were required to meet four of the following five criteria:

1. School dropout.
2. Unemployed head of household.
3. Income less than $3,000 in the past 12 months.
4. Poor work history.
5. No primary working skills.

No psychological tests were administered to the trainees at any time in the selection process; it was felt that they would be hostile to the use of tests and would respond with distrust and dislike of the program.

Applicants were obtained by referral from 33 different agencies in the San Francisco-Sunnyvale area. The agencies furnishing the largest number of accepted trainees included the Urban League, the Mexican-American Opportunities Center, the Opportunities Industrialization Center West, and the Skills Centers.

The only major problem encountered in recruitment was the failure to obtain enough trainees who were "hard" enough to qualify for the program and have acceptable arrest records. The low unemployment rate in the Sunnyvale area and the availability of other jobs are undoubtedly factors in this situation. An increased effort to recruit more, or an easing of the qualifications for the program, appears to be a necessity.

All trainees are supposed to have taken a prevocational training course at the Opportunities Industrialization Center West or at the East Bay Skills Center. The OICW has a six-week course, but Lockheed did not require the entire six weeks; three weeks was sufficient. In fact, it was found that some of the trainees had not attended the prevocational training course and did not seem to be adversely affected. However, the utilization of the OICW was felt to have benefits for the company and the community in addition to those derived from the training. It provides community participation and obtains support from the minority organizations.

The OICW program was directed at (1) improving reading, writing, speaking, and computational skills; (2) developing good grooming, health, and hygiene habits; and (3) improving attitudes toward work.

Upon employment at Lockheed, the trainees entered one of a number of four-week courses designed specifically for a given occupation. These occupations included (1) general helper-factory, (2) electrical assembler, and (3) keypunch operator. The trainees knew they were being trained for a specific job and what it was, and they were assigned to that classification immediately.

The original plan called for the trainees to receive on-the-job training for six weeks. This has since been changed, and the trainees now have a four-week vestibule-training period followed by a six-week period, where 50 percent of the time is spent in training on the job. This is followed by a ten-week span, where 25 percent of the time is spent in on-the-job training.

The original plan also called for "training and advancement" after six months of satisfactory job performance. This has been dropped from the plan because other, more senior employees complained because they were not offered the same training.

The Vocational Improvement Program (VIP) cost $89,500 for 1967, or $860 for each trainee who completed the training. Of this, Manpower Development and Training Act (MDTA) funds covered $9,200, and Lockheed's cost was approximately $80,000, or $770 per trainee who completed the training. The MDTA funds have been used to pay for part of the instructors' salaries and some training supplies.

A number of problems arose in the training. The most persistent one was the trainees' need for assistance with their personal problems. They continually had difficulty with transportation, finances, and the law. They continually needed assistance to get their affairs straightened out and made extensive demands on the time of the training supervisor. The women had more personal problems, but they were usually of a less severe nature than those of the men and required less time to handle.

A second problem that arose was that the trainees did not learn by association; they had extremely limited associative experiences and learned much more effectively through the use of physical demonstration, especially if they could try the lesson manually. This required continual repetition until the skill was well learned and revealed one of the major reasons that training the hard core may take approximately 50 percent longer than training other employees.

Another problem was that of attendance, which proved to have two root causes. One was the transportation headache. Workers had to have automobiles to get to work. Some shared in car pools; others attempted to drive cars that were in poor mechanical condition. The second cause of absenteeism was from an unexpected source. Once the trainee joined the Lockheed workforce, a yet unknown network spread the information quite freely. This resulted in warrants being issued for back traffic violations. If the violator was on welfare, the matter was not pressed. But as soon as he became employed, the tickets were presented. This led to court appearances and loss of time from the job.

A further problem was that, to some degree, the line did not accept the program as partly theirs. Some saw it as an education and training program and failed to identify with it. To them, trainees were "education's people."

There were no special courses or programs for supervision to introduce them to the problems of hard-core employees. Shortly before the end of the training period, the supervisors came down to the training location to meet the trainees. This was accomplished in a relatively informal manner. On-the-job counseling was handled by supervisors or by the personnel representatives to whom the trainees were referred. However, despite this, some of the trainees returned to the training area to obtain additional help from either their training instructor or supervisor, or both.

Gaining union acceptance of the program required the company to completely spell out the goals of the training and required an assurance that the provisions of the union contract would not be vio-

lated. Once this hurdle was cleared, the union became most cooperative.

So that the productivity of the trainees could be evaluated, a
comparison group of 50 employees who were hired into the same
occupations at the same time were matched with 50 of the VIP trainees. The matching was very close on age, but the hard-core group
had one year less of education and two dependents more than the
comparison group. Absenteeism data and quality and quantity ratings
were then obtained on each group. The ratings obtained were gathered from the regular administrative review that is routinely obtained
for each employee each year. There was extremely little difference between the trainees and the comparison group in the ratings on quality
and quantity. In the absenteeism ratings, there was a larger proportion of trainees who had records involving numerous absences than
there was among the comparison group, but the difference was not
statistically significant over an extended period of time.

Of the 111 trainees who completed training in 1967, 16 of them
(14 percent) terminated before the end of the year. During the same
period of time, 14 percent of the comparison group terminated. The
average length of tenure at that time was just under 4.5 months; previous experience would indicate that this level of termination is extremely low. Of the 16 terminations among the hard-core trainees,
half were voluntary and the other half dismissals. Of the eight involuntary terminations, six were for excessive absenteeism, one for
absenteeism and inability to perform, and one for conviction of a
felony. In the comparison group there was a lower percentage of
voluntary, and a higher percentage of involuntary, terminations.

Retention rate of the starting group is considered good. Of the
111 who started in 1967, 95 completed the first year. In April 1969,
68 were still on the company's payroll, 20 of whom were on layoff but
eligible for recall.

At the end of the first year, a "follow-up questionnaire" was completed by having the instructors question the trainees' supervisors.
Some supervisors had their people for a very short period of time (30
days), others for as much as six months. The two most frequent comments from the supervisors concerned poor attendance and lack of
blueprint-reading skill (a skill not required for the job but a requirement for normal progression into better jobs). There was very little
evidence of inability to perform the occupation being carried out or
inability to adjust to supervision and fellow workers.

The major alterations to the original 1967 program are listed below:

- *The company has employed a full-time counselor.* The trainees have consistently required a large amount of the time of the training supervisor who is in charge of the program in their attempts to obtain guidance and/or assistance with personal and vocational problems. These problems interfere with their training to a great enough degree that it is felt that someone should be responsible for providing such assistance.
- *Counseling services from community agencies were obtained.* Some of the problems that arise can be handled more effectively by representatives from such agencies as the Urban League, the Mexican-American Opportunities Center, and the California State Employment Service. These agencies have agreed to provide representatives at the plant to make their services more available to the trainees.
- *A course dealing with problems of supervising minority disadvantaged workers was developed for supervisors.* Experience indicates that many members of management and supervision are unable to communicate effectively with the minority disadvantaged worker because they do not understand his culture and his attitudes. A course on human relations with minority personnel was, therefore, developed for presentation to managers and supervisors in those areas receiving hard-core trainees.
- *The trainees were classified as "trainees."* Having the trainees hold the classification that they will have when they go to the line after their training created some resentment, so they are now classified as trainees during their training, and then reclassified when they go to the line.
- *The OJT training period was extended.* The OJT training was extended to accomplish two objectives: (1) to obtain greater MDTA funding and (2) to provide a greater opportunity to identify and correct training and adjustment problems.

The most important things that Lockheed learned from this experience were to—

1. Train the trainees specifically for the job and insure that the trainees see the connection.
2. Develop self-confidence in the trainees. Break the tasks down into small portions and give rewards frequently. Look for opportunities to compliment their work.
3. Teach by demonstration and repetition. The trainees have poor associative networks and, therefore, do not learn well by association.
4. Require good work habits throughout training; don't let poor habits get established.
5. Provide financial, vocational, and personal counseling and advice as required.
6. Recognize the existence of individual differences.
7. Train to a higher standard than required by the line, to increase line acceptance.
8. Keep student-teacher ratio small—preferably 1:5.

Lockheed found that in hiring heads of households it obtained an extra factor of built-in self-motivation. Further, the Lockheed plan was designed so that the trainee had a job and was on the Lockheed payroll the day he began his training. This knowledge increased motivation and was considered responsible for the low dropout rate.

The disadvantaged know extremely little about the jobs that are available in industry or how to qualify for them. The Lockheed program was successful in training disadvantaged personnel to perform successfully in industrial jobs. And, from my investigation, I believe that three other important elements contributed heavily to this success:

1. The personnel responsible for the programs are committed to that objective. They committed themselves to doing their best job, not just one that was acceptable to the corporate office.
2. All personnel involved cared about the trainees as people and provided whatever assistance was necessary to aid the trainees in handling whatever problems arose. At Lockheed's Sunnyvale plant it became almost routine to bail men out of jail, assist in transportation, help people solve financial problems, and so forth.

3. The training was directed specifically at *a* job, and the trainees were required to attain a standard greater than the minimum required for that job during their training.

Exhibit 10. *"Profile of Trainees"; Excerpt Prepared by the Author from a Training Manual Used in Preparing Foremen to Receive Hard-Core Trainees in Their Sections at Pacific Telephone and Telegraph*

CHARACTERISTIC	BELIEFS	PROBABLE BEHAVIOR
Lack of self-confidence.	That they will be unsuccessful in any task they attempt.	1. Will not apply for job. 2. Will quit if they encounter any obstacle that appears unfamiliar. 3. Will do things to avoid facing certain situations. 4. Are very sensitive and defensive of their behavior. 5. May read prejudice into a situation in order to protect self-image. May actively seek suggestions of prejudice so that they may withdraw from the situation. 6. This behavior is an attempt to avoid situations that might lead to failure.
Antibusiness.	That business still discriminates despite pronouncements. That the present flurry is merely tokenism. That black people are the "last hired and the first fired."	1. Low level of trust. 2. Constantly probing to uncover the "game." 3. Expect firms to manufacture reasons for not hiring. A few examples might be "tests" requiring a high school diploma, "loading the actual interview." 4. Expect firm to seek reasons for not promoting.

Exhibit 10 (concluded)

		5. Expect firm to seek or manufacture reasons for firing.
		6. Expect firm to show preferential treatment to whites doing same job.
Antiwhite.	That most whites are biased.	1. Submissive: Will avoid contact with whites until they demonstrate through behavior that they can be trusted not to "offend." This offensiveness takes the form of ridicule or patronage. Some blacks accept the inferior role in order to avoid rejection or "trouble."
		2. Aggressive: Usually viewed by whites as "chip on the shoulder behavior." Very sensitive to mannerisms and language of whites. Tend to avoid contact unless it is part of the job.
Feeling of inferiority.	That they are really not up to par. That maybe they are "second-class." This is a learned belief.	1. Dress, language (content and tone), and hairstyles. These expressions are overt acts to establish an identity. May also be viewed as acts of compensation, to make up for the many things that society denies to them. In the case of the "Afro" hairstyle and clothing it is an act of rejection of white values.

EXHIBIT 11. *Interdepartmental Memorandum Describing Results Planned for Trainees in the Vocational Instruction Program (VIP), Together with Appropriate Job Descriptions, at Lockheed Missiles & Space Company*

INTERDEPARTMENTAL COMMUNICATION

To

Dept./	Bldg./	Plant/	Date
Orgn.	Zone	Fac.	

From

Dept./	Bldg./	Plant/	Ext.
Orgn.	Zone	Fac.	

SUBJECT: VIP CAPABILITY AT THE END OF THE FOUR-WEEK
TRAINING PERIOD

At the end of the VIP Training Course for General Helpers-
Factory, the student will be able to

1. Add and subtract angular measurements in degrees, minutes, and seconds.
2. Add and subtract, multiply and divide whole numbers and decimals.
3. Convert decimals to fractions and fractions to decimals.
4. Construct sample three-dimensional objects, using three-view orthographic drawings.
5. Do simple flat-pattern layout of clips, brackets, and so forth, using multiview drawings as reference sources.
6. Lay out and install Huck rivet and bolt fasteners, using a multiview drawing and maintaining a tolerance of $\pm$ .030.
7. Set up and operate the 4' foot power shear, 4' leaf brake, and electric drill press.
8. Use standard sheet-metal hand tools, such as files, drills, rivet guns, and hammers.

Exhibit 11 (continued)

9. Use in a job application such precision measuring
   tools as calipers, micrometers, and squares.

On completion of the four-week training course for VIP
Electrical Assemblers, the student will be able to use to
LMSC manufacturing standards
1. Thermo-wire strippers on nylon, teflon, and poly-
   insulated wires.
2. Standard electrical shop tools, such as soldering
   irons, diagonal cutters, pliers, and heat sinks.
3. Solder multigauge wires with various insulations into
   terminal boards, pins, sockets, eyelets, and so forth.
4. Install and solder resistors, capacitors, and similar
   components to post terminals and eyelets.

GENERAL HELPER—FACTORY

OCCUPATIONAL SUMMARY:
This occupation requires the performance of miscellaneous
manual operations and assisting skilled and semiskilled
workers in the performance of their duties.

WORK PERFORMED:
Move, and help in moving or positioning, parts, assemblies,
dies, tools, equipment, fixtures or materials for the
setup and operation of various machine tools, fabrication
machines, processing or laboratory equipment.
Assist other employees in handling and positioning heavy
materials and equipment; securing tools for setup; helping
in breaking down setups, properly segregating tools and
fixtures and returning to proper sources. Load and unload
parts on and off machines. Remove scrap, shavings, or chips
from machines and help in keeping work areas and machines
and equipment clean and in orderly condition. Number or
hand-stamp parts for identification. Clean and lubricate
parts before or subsequent to operations.
Independently perform simple routine and repetitive operations, such as burring, sanding, puttying, masking, and
hand stenciling.

Exhibit 11 (concluded)

When other duties permit, helpers may be given the opportunity to learn operation of machines and equipment where
setup is made and operations are of a simple repetitive
nature or are performed under close supervision.

ELECTRICAL ASSEMBLER

OCCUPATIONAL SUMMARY:
This occupation requires the performance of a variety of
basic soldering relative to wire fabrication and electrical
and electronic assembly operations where planning and
sequencing of operations have been determined and supported
by clearly defined operation sheets and instructions.

WORK PERFORMED:
Install and solder electrical and electronic components,
such as jumper wire, capacitors, resistors, multipin con-
nectors, printed-circuit board, and terminal-board type of
wiring from complete information where operations have been
reduced to judgments of direct numerical or pictorial
identification. Perform continuity checks required by the
work described herein.
Perform minor mechanical or electrical assembling operations, such as installing, assembling, and disassembling
plugs, switches, and other similar accessories; wire
preparations, such as grouping, tagging, stripping, and
tinning in sets for assembly; making up terminal strips and
bonding braids.
Set up and operate lugging, wire numbering, stripping,
cutting, stamping machines, and swaging equipment.
Work from clearly defined wiring diagrams, illustrations,
or wire cards where the components and location are
specified.
Perform rework of the same level of difficulty as other
work described herein.
Must pass soldering test for certification.
Assist the Electrical Assembler-Senior as required.
Use all the tools, materials, and equipment necessary to
complete the job and must be familiar with simple
arithmetic.

EXHIBIT 12. *Description of MA-4 Training Methodology at Education and Technical Services Division of Philco-Ford*

PROGRAM CONTENT AND METHODOLOGY

1. SUMMARY PROGRAM DESCRIPTION

The total proposed training program has been developed around the premise that all program components must relate to job preparation and retention of the employee/trainee. Instructional strategies are based upon initial assessment and evaluation of the individual. The training program will be tailored to offer maximum remediation for job-related basic education skills, through use of materials that are job-relevant.

The "real" teaching approach is stressed—that is, "real" problems are encountered and mastered, "real" pay checks are used as a basis to compute deductions, "real types" of supervisory situations are introduced so that the employee/trainee becomes accustomed to work situations and expectations.

Prevocational training and counseling stress the "real" world of work: knowledge of fundamentals, experience with policies and procedures, discussion of employer-employee relationships, and employee-supervisor attitudes.

The total training experience is designed to give each trainee a "leg up" to employment and to help him psychologically, educationally, and vocationally to feel, as well as to become, capable of handling and holding the job.

2. SELECTION

Selection will be based upon an initial interview and evaluation by Philco-Ford following testing by an independent agency, whenever possible, to
- Arrive at an assessment of individual capacities, in relationship to available job openings.
- Fit the individual to the job that appears best suited to his capabilities.
- Evaluate skills, attitudes, and aptitudes most in need of reinforcement.
- Screen candidates for possible referral to other programs because of physical incapacity or ineducability.

Exhibit 12 (continued)

It is expected that the majority of candidates will be
selected for entry into the program and placed on jobs.
The selection process is primarily designed to fit the
individual to the job for which he appears to have the most
potential for sustained employment. Medical examinations
will be given at this time to determine physical capability
for employment.

Candidates who are screened will have received prior
certification for eligibility from the State Employment
Service.

3. ORIENTATION

The orientation portion of the training program is designed to acquaint employee/trainees with general policies
and procedures in the world of work, to assess further
their educational level, and to reinforce basic communications and computational skills. It is intended, furthermore, to provide intensive counseling opportunities.

Newly arrived employee/trainees will be informed of what
to expect in the training program, of what is expected of
them, and what successful completion can mean, personally
and in terms of economics. The orientation will strive to
be motivational while, at the same time, will present the
need for self-discipline and responsibility on the part
of the trainee.

The curriculum for the orientation program will include
experiences with general business forms, printed policies,
and payroll information all employees/trainees will en-
counter. Moreover, the reading and computational skills will
be mastered in relationship to their world-of-work application. Counseling will emphasize general expectations of
employers, attitudes of fellow employees, and employment
problems faced previously by employee/trainees. These will
form the basis for initial group counseling, which will
show how some of the problems could have been avoided, or
alleviated in early stages. Positive learning will emanate
from this background.

4. JOB-RELATED BASIC AND PREVOCATIONAL EDUCATION

Training in basic and prevocational education involves

Exhibit 12 (continued)

acquisition of skill and proficiency in reading, writing, communicating, and computing, and an orientation to selected vocational areas. Training content is derived from the world of work; the level to be attained is that necessary to function and benefit from an OJT training situation.

Materials used in reading and writing are work-related: instruction manuals, plan sheets, and work orders. Writing skills will deal with forms, time cards, and work estimates, to cope with necessary business paperwork. Communication involves ability to receive and understand written and oral job instructions, to report work progress, to exchange information, and to respond to direction. Prevocational training includes acquisition of vocabularies related to concrete work applications.

Functional mathematics deals with computations arising in job performance; basic skills in numerical manipulation, such as measurement, areas, weights, and estimates of time and materials; training in fractions, decimals, and percentages as related to job performance, budgeting, and consumer education.

Prevocational training introduces trainees to a broad spectrum of materials, tools, and equipment common to job assignments. Shop practices and procedures, including safety aspects, are covered. Training is conducted in a simulated work setting, with forms, materials, tools, and equipment used that reflect those currently in use in business and industry.

5. COUNSELING AND ATTITUDINAL TRAINING

Attitudinal training is based on responsibility. The trainee is made aware of his responsibility—to his employer, to his job, to his fellow employees, and to himself. The trainee learns of the obligations inherent in holding a job; he sees what the employer expects of him. Punctuality, courtesy, acceptance of criticism, and ready response to direction are instilled. Attitudes are directed to pride in work as part of a team.

Counseling deals with creation of a desirable self-image, fostering positive work attitudes and behavior, and elimination of employment problems.

Exhibit 12 (continued)

6. ON-THE-JOB TRAINING

On-the-job training will commence at the end of job-related basic education. OJT will build upon the prevocational base of knowledge that the employee/trainee has gained in his prior training. On-the-job training is designed to permit the employee to learn the specific skills needed in his particular job location. His training is individually tailored by the employing concern so that he may be assured of meeting the specific requirements of the job.

Counselors will make periodic visits to the OJT locations to assist supervisors and to offer support and encouragement to employees. It is expected that the prior attitudinal training will enable the employee to enter OJT motivated and receptive so that he may benefit from effective training and sustained employment.

After the trainee has been placed in the classic OJT situation, he will be furnished a continued ongoing counseling service to assist him in overcoming unforeseen situations. In many cases it is anticipated that his return to the prevocational training facility may be necessary. These services will be provided as required, either at the employers facility or at the prevocational facility by the subcontractor.

7. EMPLOYER SENSITIVITY TRAINING

Shop foremen and other supervisory personnel who will deal directly with the trainees may be provided with sensitivity training. The basic orientation will be directed toward an understanding of the problems and needs of the target population, encouragement to view the trainees as individuals, and assisting the supervisor in assuming the teaching role.

Group discussion sessions will be arranged in which supervisory personnel can receive guidance and orientation from the counselors. Problems and attitudes can be brought to light; and, in peer-group participation, solutions can be sought, which will have direct application. Techniques and methods can be examined and explained in this supportive peer-group environment.

Through discussion and role playing directed by the

Exhibit 12 (continued)

counselor, the foreman can learn techniques of instruction, how to direct the new employee, how to assess and evaluate his job performance, and how to encourage and sustain him in his efforts. Discussion can bring to light the value of realistic criticism and, equally important, the value of realistic praise and encouragement.

The following course outlines contain materials that will be utilized in conducting employer sensitivity training for this program.

UNDERSTANDING YOUR NEW EMPLOYEE: HIS BACKGROUND AND PROBLEMS

- Inadequate levels of education and specific skills.
- Transportation—cost, distance, poor facilities.
- Health problems.
- Self-image.
- Societal attitudes.
- Work attitudes.
- Materials dealing with NAB partnership and job opportunities in the business sector.

HOW THE NEW EMPLOYEE CAN HELP YOU

- Utilize human resources.
- More people at work.
- Better company image.
- Expanded business.

SYSTEMS OF HANDLING AND HELPING THE NEW EMPLOYEE

- Buddy system.
- Father or mother identity figure.
- The confidante.
- Group or class plan.
- Counseling the new employee.
  Unacceptable behaviorisms frequently found among the hard-core unemployed.
- The attitude of the counselor.

SUPERVISING THE NEW EMPLOYEE

- Creating the growth environment.
- What all workers want.
- Principles of organization in the growth environment.

Exhibit 12 (continued)

EFFECTIVE USE OF EMPLOYEE

- The right employee on the right job.
- Helping the employee maintain his availability for work.
- How well do you know your community?
- Stimulate the employee to work.
- Follow-up on employee adjustment.
- Increase the employee's capacity to work.
- How to handle problem employees.
     Mental health vs. production.
     Behavior patterns.
     Counseling the problem employee.
     Conducting the counseling session.
     Referrals are necessary.
     Discipline.
- When to use written directions.
- When to use verbal directions.

EVALUATING THE NEW EMPLOYEE

- The purpose of evaluation.
- Evaluating the new employee.
     A special file.
- Considerate supervision.

THE SUPERVISOR LOOKS AT HIMSELF

- Evaluation questions.
- Improved company morale.
- Healthy and proud nation.

HOW THE SUPERVISOR CAN HELP

- The value of work in human development.
- Family is basic.
- The nature of job adjustment.
- The areas of job adjustment.
- Interpersonal relations.
     Worker to the supervisor.
     Worker to other workers as individuals.
     Worker to the group as a whole.
- The use of abilities.
- Work satisfaction.

Exhibit 12 (continued)

- Adaptation to work pressures.
- Behavior as a worker.
- Predicting job adjustment.
- Orientation to reality.
- The meaning of work.
- Adequate minimum abilities.
- Acceptance of work.
- Starting the new employee on his job.

ORIENTATION PROGRAMS FOR THE NEW EMPLOYEE
- A friendly greeter.
    Know the new employee.
    Personalized name tag.
    "Welcome" bulletin boards.
    Meet important people.
    Coffee break and lunch with others.
    Handle the mechanics of beginnings slowly and carefully.
    Give him a tour of the plant or building.
    Welcome him back.
- The continuing orientation program.
    You and the job.
    Grooming and hygiene.
    Money management, consumer economics.
    Transportation (getting to work and so on).
    Job preparation.
    Attitudes and your job.
    Human relations.
    The tomorrow of your job.
    Expressing your problems.
    Developing person and contributing to life.
- Characteristics of a good leader.
- Supervisor's inventory.
- The unsuccessful supervisor.

8. HEALTH
   During the selection process, each trainee candidate will
be given a medical and dental examination to determine his
physical fitness for full-time employment. When such examination reveals correctable minor defects, such as
glasses requirement, light dental work; i.e., tooth filling,

Exhibit 12 (concluded)

corrective shoes, and similar nonincapacitating ailments,
the subcontractor will make arrangements to have same
corrected. Care will be taken to insure that each trainee
who enters the program will be physically able to perform
work at his position. Trainee candidates with major physical
defects will be referred to local community health centers
for assistance.

9. RECRUITMENT

Coordination with the State Employment Security Commission will be developed into an ongoing program function.
All potential trainees will be processed through the state
agency to determine eligibility for the program. Recruitment will be a joint prime contractor-Employment Service
function.

The prime contractor, with assistance of the training
subcontractor, will conduct intensive recruitment programs.
The recruitment effort will be multilateral in scope: The
aid of local community and religious organizations will be
enlisted. All individuals not initially recruited by the
State Employment Service will then be referred to them for
certification.

Exhibit 13. *Orientation Schedule for Hard-Core Unemployed at Xerox Corporation*

XEROX TRAINING PROGRAM—"HARD CORE" UNEMPLOYED
ORIENTATION SCHEDULE

Types and Length of Activities

Hours	Activities
1	Welcome by various company representatives
3	Explanation and discussion of training program
½	Xerox Routine—badges, safety glasses, A/L procedures
3½	Movies with discussion
	"Don't Press Your Luck"
	"Office Safety"
	Caterpillar Safety Movie
	Joe Wilson Movie
	"Company for Lunch"
	"What's It All About?"
	Xerox products—slides
	"Ahead With the 2400 Machine"
	"Safety Makes Sense"
2	Explanation of Xerox policies and benefits
1	Responsibilities of employee-trainee
½	Explanation of work assignments and work areas
2	Facts about the company and machine demonstration
1	Tour of manufacturing area
2½	Safety presentation and safety shoes
1	Materials-handling presentation
½	Introduction to community worker
1	Discussion of trainee's future (former trainee & counselor)
1	Rules of conduct
2	Achievement tests
1	Introduction of union representative and industrial relations representative

EXHIBIT 14. *Excerpts from Xerox Corporation (Rochester) Orientation for New Hard-Core Trainees*

INDUSTRIAL ORIENTATION
INDUSTRIAL RELATIONSHIPS

Aim: To contribute to the development of the trainees' work
   attitudes through group discussions of their obligations
   to Xerox, attitudes of other employees, plus a review of
   shop rules and corresponding disciplinary actions.

Motivation: The sessions are introduced through a discussion with the trainees relating to the importance of
   recognizing the shop rules and their application. The
   sessions are very informal, with all material being
   presented through group discussion. The discussion leader
   may provide additional background detail as to some of his
   experience with cases in the plant.

Development:
   Session I: A discussion of "What Xerox Owes Each
      Employee?"
      (A trainee records answers on the blackboard.)
         Items discussed by the group are
            Salaries as good as other companies
            Benefits to cover emergencies
            Safe working conditions
            The opportunity to develop and learn new skills
            The opportunity for promotion
            Pleasant work surroundings
            Up-to-date safe working equipment
   Following this a discussion is held on "What the
      Trainee Owes Xerox?"
   (Again, an employee records information.)
      Some items that are reviewed are as follows:
         Work in a safe manner
         A good record of absence and lateness
         To learn new skills and develop as an employee
         Work as a member of a team with good relationships
            with other employees
   Session II: The film of the two white employees discuss-

Exhibit 14 (continued)

ing the problems in the shop when "hard core" employees
are hired is viewed and discussed. Attention is given
to how the trainee should react if confronted with
"racist" attitudes or comments.

Sessions III & IV: The trainees are asked what rules they
feel a company needs to maintain order in a plant to
assure effective production. The discussion is handled
by placing the trainees in the role of owning or running
the plant; they discuss what rules they would impose.
A record of the rules is made on the board.
Following this, the remainder of III and IV is spent in
discussing the actual rules and why each is an important
rule and the disciplinary action in which violation of
the rule can result. Again the trainee is asked to
place himself in the role of the foreman or man
running the plant. For example, "If you were the foreman, why do you feel you would need rules about wearing safety glasses? What would you do as foreman if I,
your employee, continued to violate the rule on
safety glasses?"

INDUSTRIAL ORIENTATION
PERSONAL FINANCE

1. Garnishment—This lesson was used for a twofold reason:
   to introduce a series on finance and also to explain
   how it happens to an individual and how one is affected
   by company policy. The following points were covered:
   income executions, wage assignments (garnishments),
   repossessions, and collection agencies. Also covered
   was what you can do if you get a garnishment.
2. Fraudulent Selling—This lesson presented the point that
   fraud suggests deception and trickery. Examples of
   fraudulent and deceptive selling practices were discussed. The aim of the lesson was to develop an awareness of some fraudulent and deceptive selling practices
   and also to acquaint the class with the state publication "The Ten-Point Buying Guide for Consumers."

Exhibit 14 (concluded)

3. Buying on Time—The aim of this lesson was to establish some guidelines for buying on time and to develop an understanding that credit costs money. It was pointed out that easy credit has encouraged many families to take on more debts than they can handle. The cost of credit and the different types of credit were covered.
4. Shopping for Money—In this lesson the following points were taught to the trainees: We tried to acquaint the students with the lowest cost sources for credit, familiarize the class with the various kinds of lending agencies, and to help the trainees protect themselves against unscrupulous lenders.
5. Banking Services—In this lesson our aim was to familiarize the trainees with banks and their services and also to develop the habit of saving money. The many financial services offered by the bank to the family were discussed and then an additional hour was spent on a tour of the Marine Midland Branch Bank in Webster.

INDUSTRIAL ORIENTATION
GENERAL SAFETY PRESENTATION

Aim: To demonstrate the correct methods in material handling.

The following situations were discussed or demonstrated:
  A. Manpower—how to lift properly
  B. Equipment—hoists, rollers, trucks, blocking of trucks
  C. Stocking—neatness, stability of load
  D. Aisles—keep open—importance
  E. Smoking—fire hazards
  F. Rubbish—own work area
  G. Special Materials—acids, solvents, chemicals in general

A filmstrip on proper lifting was used to promote discussion.

EXHIBIT 15. *Form Used by AVCO Economic Systems Corporation, Roxbury Division, to Show Details Relating to Termination of Individual Training*

INDIVIDUAL TRAINEE TERMINATION
TRAINING OR SERVICES

FORM APPROVED
BUDGET BUREAU NO. 44-R1204.1

PROGRAM:	PROJECT:	TRNG. PHASE:
MDTA ——1	INST.——1	OCCUPATIONAL ——0
RAR ——2	OJT ——2	BASIC ED. ——1
OTHER——3	E&D ——4	PRE-VOC. ——2
NYC ——4		OTHER ——4

A. 1. NAME - LAST, FIRST, MIDDLE INITIAL   2. SOCIAL SECURITY NO.   3. SEX (CHECK ONE) M   F

ADDRESS - STREET, CITY, STATE

B. 1. STATE   2. PROJECT   3. SECTION (MDTA & RAR   4. OCCUP. GOAL OR SERVICE FURNISHED
(NAME AND CODE)   NUMBER   NUMBER ONLY)

5. FIRST DAY ATTENDED	6. LAST DAY ATTENDED	7. NO. DAYS	8. NO. DAYS	9. CLOCK HOURS
MONTH DAY YEAR	MONTH DAY YEAR	ATTENDED	ABSENT	ATTENDED

C. 1. NATURE OF TERMINATION   **C. 2. TRANSFERRED TO: (NYC ONLY)**

COMPLETED FULL COURSE ——00	DID NOT COMPLETE	VOCATIONAL TRAINING——11	OTHER SCHOOL ——14
EARLY COMPLETION ——01	COURSE:	APPRENTICESHIP TRNG——12	OTHER NYC PROJECT——15
ACHIEVED TRAINING OBJECTIVE	INVOLUNTARY ——03	REGULAR SCHOOL ——13	UNKNOWN ——16
PRIOR TO END OF COURSE ——02	VOLUNTARY ——04		

D. EXISTING CONDITIONS AT TIME OF TERMINATION

1. IF TRAINEE DID NOT COMPLETE, INDICATE CONDITION BY CHECK. IF MORE THAN ONE CONDITION PRESENT, CHECK ALL APPLICABLE CONDITIONS AND CIRCLE ONE MOST IMPORTANT CONDITION.

POOR ATTENDANCE ——30	MOVED FROM AREA ——36	TRANSPORTATION PROBLEMS ——42	DISLIKED COUNSELOR——54
LACK OF PROGRESS ——31	CARE FOR FAMILY ——37	ENTERED ARMED FORCES ——43	AGREEMENT TERM ——55
MISCONDUCT ——32	PREGNANCY OF TRNEE. ——38	COULDN'T ADJ. TO TRNG/WRK——50	UNKNOWN ——56
ALCOHOLISM ——33	ILLNESS OF TRAINEE ——39	LOST INTEREST ——51	OTHER (SPECIFY) ——57
COMMITTED TO INST.——34	FULL-TIME SCHOOL ——40	DIDN'T ATT. REMED'L CLASS ——52	
POOR HOURS OR LOC.——35	INSUF. PAY OR ALLOW.——41	DISLIKED INSTRUCTOR ——53	

2. WAS TRAINEE INTERVIEWED BEFORE THIS SECTION WAS COMPLETED?   YES——1.   NO——2.

E. STATUS AT TIME OF TERMINATION (COMPLETE FOR ALL TRAINEES; CHECK ONE)

WORKING OR SCHEDULED TO REPORT TO: NOT SCHEDULED TO REPORT TO A JOB BUT:

TRAINING RELATED JOB ——01	LOOKING FOR WORK ——03	SCHEDULED FOR FURTHER TRNG.——05
NON-TRAINING RELATED JOB——02	NOT LOOKING FOR WORK——04	NOT KNOWN ——06

F. FOR THE TRAINING FACILITY (COMPLETE FOR MDTA TRAINEES ONLY; CHECK ONE)

DATE:_____

THIS IS TO CERTIFY THAT THE CIRCUMSTANCES OF TERMINATION FOR THE TRAINEE TO WHOM THIS REPORT REFERS ARE:

FOR GOOD CAUSE_____1.   NOT FOR GOOD CAUSE_____2.

NAME: (SIGNATURE) _____ (FACILITY NAME)_____

(TYPED OR PRINTED)_____ ADDRESS _____

TITLE _____

G. FACILITY OR DEPT. HEAD REVIEW (COMPLETE FOR NYC. FOR MDTA COMPLETE IF TERMINATION WAS NOT FOR GOOD CAUSE)

I HAVE REVIEWED THE CIRCUMSTANCES SURROUNDING THE TERMINATION OF THE TRAINEE TO WHICH THIS REPORT REFERS AND HAVE FOUND THEM TO BE ACCURATELY DESCRIBED.

NAME: (SIGNATURE)_____ TITLE: (AGENCY HEAD)_____

(TYPED OR PRINTED)_____ AGENCY NAME _____

H. FOR USE BY SELECTION OR REFERRAL OFFICE (CHECK APPLICABLE ITEMS)

1. ALL PHASES OF TRAINING OR SERVICES TERMINATED: YES——1 NO——2

2A. IF NO, ADDITIONAL OR CONTINUING ACTIVITY SCHEDULED: B. PROJECT NO._____ C. SECTION NO. _____

MDTA ——1	INST.——1	OCCUPATIONAL——0
RAR ——2	OJT ——2	BASIC ED. ——1
OTHER——3	E&D ——4	PRE-VOC. ——2
NYC ——4		OTHER ——4

D. OCCUPATION _____ DOT CODE _____

E. TRAINEE ENROLLED IN ADDITIONAL ACTIVITY;

YES——1 NO——2

F. IF NOT ENROLLED, ENTER COND. CODE (SEC. D.1.)_____

G. GOOD CAUSE: YES——1 NO——2

STATE NAME AND CODE_____ OFFICE OR AGREEMENT NO._____ DATE_____

EXHIBIT 16. *Memorandum Outlining Case History of Employing the Hard-Core Unemployed at a Life Insurance Company* (The company has asked to remain anonymous.)

DATE: April 7, 1969

For:

                              PERSONNEL DEPARTMENT

SUBJECT: Pilot JOBS Skill Training Program: A Report

I. Introduction

Before joining the Personnel Department on September 9, 1968, I presented a design for a pilot JOBS Skill Training Program to the second vice president, which he approved. The program was designed as yet one more component of our over-all commitment to the National Alliance of Businessmen to hire, train, and retain 150 otherwise unemployable persons during the one-year period that began in June, 1968.

The JOBS Skill Training Program is designed to last 16 weeks, during which time trainees are in class half of each workday and on a real job the other half of each workday. Its four chief foci are (1) Orientation to the World of Work at the company, (2) the development of a specific job skill for which the company now has a real need (typing and calculating are examples), (3) the improvement of basic reading and arithmetic skills, and (4) on-the-job training. Instructorial help and curriculum content include a "mix" to be drawn from an outside agency; our own personnel (instructor-counselors for in-class training and counseling and selected supervisors for on-the-job training); the company's employee handbook and Mind, Inc.'s programmed basic education and skill training materials supplemented by such additional materials as instructor-counselors choose.

At the time I designed the program, I felt that it offered both the company and the unemployed a number of advantages. First, it provides, through a one-week orientation program, for a bridge from the ghetto world of the unemployed to the world of work at the company. Second, it offers the trainee specific skill training in typing and calculating, and the company needs such skills. Third, it offers the trainee a chance to improve his basic knowledge in reading and arithmetic. Fourth, it provides for classroom instruction to be supplemented by on-the-job

Exhibit 16 (continued)

training. Fifth, it provides for counseling of trainees and
their supervisors to stop minor problems from blowing up
into major crises. Finally, it provides its own built-in
evaluative mechanism; and, when proven successful, this
program is readily adaptable to future 16-week trainee programs for such other jobs as general clerks or, possibly,
keypunch operators.

Fifteen women started in the pilot JOBS Skill Training Program for typists on November 4, 1968. Of the 15 who started
on November 4, 1968, 13 (86.7 percent) graduated from the
program on February 27, 1969, and all 13 appear to have
been successfully placed in full-time typing jobs. This
report on our experience with the pilot class appears,
therefore, to be very much in order.

II. Interviewing and Selection

Applicants were referred to us by the Manpower and Career
Development Agency of the City of New York (referred to
hereafter as MCDA), which has previously referred applicants
to us for our high school equivalency class. The selection
criteria included (1) certification by the agency that the
applicant was eligible for the National Alliance of
Businessmen's JOBS Program, (2) a minimum of a fifth-grade
reading and fourth-grade arithmetic achievement level,
(3) a typing speed of at least 20 words per minute, (4) a
medical examination, (5) the exclusion of persons with
proven narcotics and certain sex offenses, and (6) an understanding of the program and the motivation to pursue it.
The starting salary offered was $65 weekly, with a $5
weekly increase to be given when a trainee passed the
typing test and an additional $5 weekly increase to be given
when a trainee transferred to a permanent job in an
operating department.

From October 7 through October 23, 1968, we interviewed 57
applicants, all of whom were prescreened on arrival at our
home office by an interviewer from MCDA. Of those interviewed, we hired 18 (31.6 percent), 16 for the JOBS
Skill Training Program and 2 for full-time jobs. One of
the 16 applicants who were offered training positions did
not report to work. Of the 40 applicants rejected, the sole
reason for rejection was that their typing speed was below
20 words per minute.

Exhibit 16 (continued)

All fifteen trainees who started on November 4, 1968, were
women; four were Puerto Rican, one was Mexican-American,
and ten were Negroes. Six of the women were married and the
remaining nine single; ten had one or more dependents and
five had no dependents. Twelve reside in Brooklyn, two
in Manhattan, and one in the Bronx. Seven had completed
twelve years of school, six had eleven years of school, and
two had ten years of school.

Before referral to the company, MCDA administered two tests
to measure educational achievement levels, the Gates Reading Survey and the arithmetic section of the Wide Range
Achievement Test. The average grade-achievement level in
reading was 8.5; the average grade-achievement level in
arithmetic was 6.3. The highest grade-achievement level in
reading was 11.3, the lowest 6.0. The highest grade-
achievement level in arithmetic was 9.5, the lowest 4.4.

All trainees were given our typing test at the time they
applied for the training position. Their average typing
speed was 25.9 w.p.m. The highest typing speed was 39
w.p.m.; the lowest 20 w.p.m.

All trainees were given Form A of the Adult Basic Learning
Examination[1] on November 6, 1968, their second day in training. Their average grade levels and the lowest grade levels
were

	Average[2]	Lowest
Vocabulary	9.0+	6.9
Reading	8.4	6.1
Spelling	9.0+	4.3
Arithmetic Computation	6.4	3.2
Arithmetic Problem Solving	7.4	0
Total Arithmetic Score	6.6	4.8

III. Orientation

Since Election Day fell on November 5, 1968, trainees received four days of Orientation to the World of Work at the

---

[1] Published by Harcourt, Brace, and World, and recommended
for this purpose by Dr. Samuel Ball, of Teachers College,
Columbia University.

[2] The grade-equivalent conversion table for the ABLE test
stops at 9th-grade level. Grade equivalents for raw scores
above 9th-grade level are shown in this report as 9.0+.

Exhibit 16 (continued)

company during their first week of employment. The
morning of their first day, they got to know one another
and the training staff; they were formally welcomed by Mr.
——, toured the Training Center and the Employees' Cafeteria
and Restaurant, and were briefed on the lunch period and
lunch facilities. In the afternoon, trainees were briefed
on the content of the training program, toured the building,
were briefed on attendance and punctuality standards and
how to report absences, and all had a chance to discuss the
day's highlights and consider the next day's program.
The morning of the second day and a part of the afternoon
were devoted to taking the Adult Basic Learning Examination
and completing attitude and personality surveys. The balance of the afternoon was devoted to the business of the
company.
During the morning of the third day, Dr. —— met with the
trainees for two hours on the subject "Your Health"; during
the afternoon the subject of employee rights, including the
subject of group benefits, and employee responsibilities
was discussed.
During the fourth and final day of orientation week, Mind,
Inc.'s Basic Education and Typing Curricula were introduced. Class schedules were published, "mock" classes conducted; and, finally, Mr. —— introduced the subject of
employee-supervisor and employee-employee relationships
through role playing. Each trainee was given time at the
end of the fourth day to prepare written comments on his
experiences during orientation week.
On Friday afternoons during the 15 weeks subsequent to
orientation week, group sessions were held during which
such subjects as consumer economics, housing, grooming and
make-up, and telephone techniques were covered. In addition, during Friday afternoon sessions, the staff availed
itself of the opportunity to obtain feedback from the group
concerning its experiences in the classroom and on the job.
The two supervisors of on-the-job training from the Home
Office Administration Department regularly attended these
Friday afternoon group sessions.

IV. Skill Training

The vehicle for skill training was a formal, daily, one-
hour typing class conducted for us by the training staff of

Exhibit 16 (continued)

the Employment and Training Division under Miss ——'s
direction. Difficulty was encountered with Mind, Inc.'s
audio typing program, probably due to the fact that the
trainees were relatively advanced in typing and found it
hard to adjust to the rhythmic demands of Mind's program.
More traditional teaching techniques proved effective. Two
trainees passed the typing test as early as December 5,
1968, during their fifth week of training. All had passed
the typing test by January 21, 1969, during the twelfth
week of training.

V. Basic Education

At first, classes in Language Skills (vocabulary, reading,
and spelling) and Mathematics were conducted by Mr. ——,
who had previously spent one week at Mind, Inc. headquarters office in Greenwich, Connecticut, training in the
use of the curricula materials. In January 1969, Miss ——
was employed as an instructor-counselor and, after similar
training in—————— , took over the classes from Mr. ——
so that he could give more time to counseling and
assisting with planning.

Trainees at the outset were divided into two groups (Groups
A and B) as clearly homogeneous as possible on the basis of
their educational achievement level, Group A at the lower,
Group B at the higher level. Miss —— has made the following perceptive comment on the rivalry that developed between the two groups:

> Group A developed a sense of rivalry with Group B and
> vice versa because it is natural in such an environment
> for competition to develop, and if skillfully handled, it
> can be an incentive. The fact that they were all women
> also stimulated their competitive spirit. I feel that
> emphasis should be placed on the fact that the groups
> were very close within themselves and classroom com-
> petition had very positive effects. The girls were
> patient and friendly with one another. And they were
> always willing to help one another. They developed the
> smoothest ability to criticize without offending that
> I've ever witnessed. I would also like to say that there
> was no malice between the groups; they merely adjusted
> to their division.

Both groups applied themselves quite seriously to the basic
education program. Mind, Inc.'s program in Mathematics

Exhibit 16 (continued)

proved especially useful. Its program for Language Skills
less so.
Form B of the Adult Basic Learning Examination was given to
the trainees at the conclusion of their training on
February 25, 1969.
The average grade levels and lowest grade levels on the
second test and the changes that occurred are

	Average	Change from 1st Test	Lowest	Change from 1st Test	Greatest Gain by Grade Level[3]
Vocabulary	8.2	−0.8	5.4	−1.4	1.4+
Reading	8.7	0.3	6.9	0.8	2.3
Spelling	9.0+	0	4.8	0.5	2.0+
Arithmetic Computation	7.6	1.3	4.6	0.4	2.4
Arithmetic Problem Solving	7.5	0.1	4.6	4.6[4]	1.2+
Total Arithmetic Score	7.6	1.0	5.0	0.2	1.6

VI. On-the-Job Training

On-the-job training was conducted by the Reproduction
Division of the Home Office Administration Department.
Since there were not enough extra typing stations open in
the Reproduction Division, trainees could not receive
on-the-job training there. Typewriters were set up in the
Activities Room in the basement. The Reproduction Division
supplied the supervision—Miss —— and Miss —— —and the work
to be done—fill in and copy typing. On-the-job training ran
smoothly with two exceptions. Some difficulties were encountered with porter service to set up and take down
typing tables in the Activities Room daily and some incon-

---

[3] A plus to the right of any figure in this column indicates
a pretest score below 9th-grade level and a posttest score
above 9th-grade level. See Footnote 2.
[4] One trainee had no problems correct on the first test; she
dropped out of the program before the second test was
administered.

Exhibit 16 (continued)

venience was caused other users of the Activities Room.
These were minor. Perhaps more important is a problem that
Miss —— identifies as follows:

> This phase of the program had an inflexibility to it that
> marred what could have been a wholly positive experience
> for the trainees. Trainees had one real complaint: If
> the operating departments where they were ultimately to
> work had electric typewriters there, they felt that they
> should be trained on the same. Training continued exclu-
> sively on manual typewriters. As a result, a lot of them
> lost speed during the transition to their departments
> because they were totally unfamiliar with the electric
> typewriter. I feel this deserves comment because the
> psychological effect of making constant errors after
> having built up satisfactory skill can be more than
> minimal.

VII. Counseling

Informal counseling was provided for both (1) job-related
problems and (2) non-job-related problems, and both outside
and inside the classroom as well. Miss —— has observed
that "counseling has been as effective in the classroom as
out; trainees really benefit from sincere interest when
they are troubled."

Considerable emphasis, both in group discussions and in
individual conferences, was placed on attendance and punctuality. During the first 12 weeks[5] the group's attendance
and punctuality record was as follows:

Number of Days of Absence					Periods of Absence			
All Reasons					All Reasons			
No.	Days	2	14.3%		No.	Periods	2	14.3%
1	Day	5	35.8%		1	Period	7	50.0%
2	Days	1	7.1%	S	2	Periods	2	14.3%
3	Days	2	14.3%			----------------------		
5	Days	1	7.1%		3	Periods	1	7.1%
------------------------------					5	Periods	1	7.1%
8	Days	2	14.3%	N.S.	7	Periods	1	7.1%
15	Days	1	7.1%					

---

[5] Records for the whole group for the thirteenth through
the sixteenth weeks are not at this time available because
many were transferred to typing jobs in operating departments during this period.

Exhibit 16 (continued)

		Latenesses	
	None	1	21.4%
S	One	2	14.3%
	Two	4	28.6%
	Three	1	7.1%
N.S.	Six	2	14.3%
	Eight	1	7.1%
	Seventeen	1	7.1%

Eleven (79 percent) had maintained reasonably satisfactory
attendance records during the first 12 weeks. One with
three periods of absence can be considered "borderline."
Two had unsatisfactory records; one of these terminated
for personal reasons on February 12, 1969, and the other
has since shown improvement. Nine (64 percent) had satisfactory punctuality records during the first 12 weeks. One
was "borderline." Four had unsatisfactory records, including
the one who terminated February 12. The three still employed need close follow-up.
Other counseling was provided in connection with supervisory
relationships, transfer to permanent jobs (which began as
early as January 27, 1969, for some where receiving departments were willing to release the trainee for daily
remedial education classes after transfer), and some
attempts were made to deal with non-job-related problems.
A follow-up counseling program is being developed for the
postgraduation period.

VIII.   Conclusions

Generally, the program appears reasonably successful, and
this became apparent fairly early. Frankly, as Miss ——
has pointed out, "We didn't allow ourselves much room for
error." The program design was used as the basis for a
contract with the United States Department of Labor for
reimbursement for expenses incurred with 90 trainees we
expect to hire in the program during 1969. However, there
are areas where improvements can be made.

   (1) Orientation: An outside agency, the Metropolitan Urban
       Service Training Facility, was retained to train our
       trainers to more effectively conduct the first week
       of orientation.

Exhibit 16 (concluded)

(2) <u>Basic</u> <u>Education</u> <u>Curriculum</u>: Efforts are now being
made to enrich the Language Skill program and, in the
case of a few trainees who are ready for it, to provide a more advanced Mathematics program. Efforts
may also be made to incorporate Mind, Inc.'s Environ-
mental Survival Skills program into the curriculum.

(3) <u>On-the-Job</u> <u>Training</u>: Future typist trainees will receive training on the electric typewriter in addition
to that on the manual typewriter.

(4) <u>Supervisors'</u> <u>Orientation</u>: A course is being developed
for first-line supervisors who receive graduates of
the program, or are to supervise on-the-job training.
The Metropolitan Urban Service Training Facility will
also assist in conducting the first of these programs.

[signed]
Executive Assistant

EXHIBIT 17. *Outline Developed by Ford Motor Company for Introducing Foremen to the Hard-Core Program, to Help Foremen Develop Plans for Helping New Hourly Employees Succeed on the
Job*

CONDUCTING MEETING

The superintendent and general foreman should act as co-
leaders, with the industrial relations supervisor providing
employment data and other related information as required.

Open meeting by stating purpose.	Refer to request made by plant manager at last meeting that foremen be brought together to develop plans for helping new employees succeed on the job.
	Tell group that this will be a prob-lem-solving meeting in which they will be asked to contribute their ideas. Point out that some ideas may require management approval and that others may be implemented immediately.

Exhibit 17 (continued)

Review highlights of plant manager's meeting.	Before proceeding with the development of plans, review highlights of the plant manager's meeting. • Company equal employment opportunity commitment. • Need to <u>productively</u> assimilate new employees into workforce. • Results of good and poor treatment of new employee by foremen and fellow employees. • Need for managers and supervisors to extend themselves because these are "unusual times."
Discuss role of foreman in helping new hires.	Mention the number of new employees who will probably be in the plant during the next few months. Emphasize help new hires will need in adjusting to fellow employees, their foremen, and what will probably be frightening surroundings. Make it clear that the company is not expecting foremen to provide extraordinary treatment to these new hires. It is expecting foremen to provide treatment that should normally be accorded <u>all</u> newly hired employees.
Review actions now being considered or implemented by some plants.	Lead group into a review of what some company locations are considering or implementing by stating that plant actions thus far have been handled either by staff departments or directly by foremen. Those programs administered by staff departments are • Transportation of New Employees. • Meal Assistance Program. • Share-a-Ride Plan. • Pre-employment Training. Actions implemented directly by foremen or involving foremen have been the following:

Exhibit 17 (continued)

	• Employee Orientation.
	• Employee Sponsor Program.
	• Telephone Campaign.
	• Job Instruction Program.
Review Orientation and Induction Card.	Hand out the pocket-size Orientation and Induction cards to the foremen. Allow enough time for group to read card.
	Solicit comments from the foremen by asking how the items on the card relate to handling of new employees on their jobs.
	List worthwhile questions on the board.
Begin problem identification.	Ask the foremen what actions not indicated on the card should be considered when "breaking in" a new employee. Questions similar to the following might be asked:
	• Should we be doing any of the things that some of the other company plants are doing—do we need any of it?
	• What suggestions do you (foremen at the meeting) have on the basis of your own experience with new hires?
	• Do any of you know of experiences that others are having with new employees?
	• Have we had any particular problems with new hires in the past?
Determining probable causes.*	After the foremen have identified problems encountered by new employees, the next step is to list <u>probable causes</u> for these problems. There may be several probable causes for each problem. Therefore, select those that

---

* Cause and solutions may be developed following each statement of a problem.

Exhibit 17 (continued)

	management or the foremen may be able to do something about.
Determine possible solutions.*	Once probable causes have been determined, direct foremen to suggest possible solutions. Encourage foremen to use their imaginations. It is not important that foremen's ideas be sophisticated or high-powered. The most effective ideas may be those that the foremen can implement themselves—immediately.
Select best solutions.	Some of the actions suggested by the foremen may require implementation by other departments in the plant. However, actions that would immediately and directly involve the foreman are to be given special attention; that is, plans for implementing these actions should be developed first. If we don't give priority to actions that the foreman can implement immediately, the employees' first three or four weeks will have escaped us and it may be too late to prevent new employee failures.
Develop plans for implementing actions.	Plans for implementing actions suggested by foremen need not be elaborately detailed. They need only specify • What action will be taken. • How it will be done. • Who will do it. • When it will be started and, if applicable, finished. Suggestions requiring approval should be prepared by the superintendent and

---

* Cause and solutions may be developed following each statement of a problem.

Exhibit 17 (continued)

general foreman with the assistance
of the industrial relations supervisor, who will forward plans to the
appropriate management personnel for
review.

Closing the
meeting.

After plans have been developed for
implementing the foremen's ideas,
the meeting should be concluded by

• Reviewing actions suggested by foremen and specifying which actions
  foremen can implement directly and
  which will require approval of plant
  management.
• Reviewing plans for implementing
  these actions and obtaining commitment from foremen specifying when
  they will implement actions that are
  within their control.
• Scheduling next meeting when foremen will
      Report on progress of actions they
      have taken.
      Be informed of management's deci-
      sions on proposals forwarded for
      review and approval.

FOLLOW-UP OF MEETINGS

Upon completion of the general foreman-foremen meetings,
the superintendent, with the assistance of the industrial
relations supervisor, should submit a report to the plant
manager combining and prioritizing plans developed by line
supervisors.

In order to assure effective implementation of the foremen's ideas, a schedule similar to the following should be
set up.

1st Week

• Conducting of general foreman-foremen meetings by
  superintendents.
• Implementing of actions by foremen that are within
  their control.

Exhibit 17 (concluded)

- Forwarding of foremen's ideas to plant management that require review and approval.

2nd Week

- Conducting of feedback meetings for general foremen and foremen informing them of plant management's decisions and establishing target dates for implementing plans approved by plant management.

REINFORCEMENT

Unless there is continuous follow-up by plant management to assure implementation of the foremen's ideas, it can be expected that many of the actions initiated as a result of this program will phase out completely and quickly. It is recognized that some of the actions may not require a continuing effort, but many will.

One method of maintaining foreman involvement is to give continuing recognition to those who contribute to the development and/or implementation of plans. This recognition may be accorded in a number of ways, such as the following:

- Congratulatory comment made by general foreman to foreman.
- Acknowledgment by superiors in presence of foreman's peers.
- Letter of commendation signed by superintendent.
- Mention of contribution in foreman's performance review.
- If appropriate, indication to foreman that his handling of new employees was factor in his being given a promotion and/or salary increase.
- When an idea suggested or implemented by a foreman as an individual or member of a group has accomplished meaningful results, the idea should be processed as a Management Proposal for commendation and/or award, if eligible.

There may be many other ways that would be more appropriate and effective than these possibilities. Regardless of the method utilized to recognize, and thereby reinforce, the foreman's behavior, it is vitally important that the recognition be given at the time the foreman takes action or shortly thereafter.

Exhibit 18. *Outline of Sensitivity Training Workshop Used by Xerox Corporation to Train First-Line Supervisors*

FOREMEN AND THE HARD CORE

I. Introduction
    "Foremen and the Hard Core" is a six-hour "sensitivity" training workshop utilized by Xerox Corporation to train first-line supervisors. The workshop serves as a training support to Project Step Up and other Xerox efforts to employ and train individuals unprepared for industry. Xerox Corporation conducts Project Step Up, a training program for the hard-core unemployed, as part of its Minority Relations Program. The workshop was developed for foremen, assistant foremen, and general foremen working in all operating sections of our Business Products Systems Manufacturing Department.
    To ensure relevancy to general supervisory training and development needs, the training session dealing with the hard core was included as part of the ongoing Supervisory Practices Workshop (SPW). SPW, a twenty-hour, ten-session program, includes training relative to labor relations, communication skills, compensation, and so on. The session, "Foremen and the Hard Core," was viewed by supervisors as a supplement to their regular training program rather than a superficially forced indoctrination program.

II. Objectives
    In order to achieve our overall goal of ensuring a productive experience for both company and hard-core workers, the following objectives were defined for our sensitivity training workshop:
    1. Increase foremen understanding of the hard core.
    2. Increase foremen awareness of the attitudes of the hard core.
    3. Increase foremen awareness of their individual positive and negative attitudes concerning the hard core.
    3. Provide a review and opportunity for practice and application of various problem-solving approaches for getting at the cause of problems.
    5. Provide an opportunity to explore the various

Exhibit 18 (continued)

aspects of the supervisor's role as an instructor.

III. Rationale

In order to achieve meaningful change and provide a maximum amount of assistance to foremen, the entire workshop was developed from the following premise:

To help individuals, we need to start with their perception of a situation.

This help is most useful if it is initially directed toward the problem causing an individual the most immediate concern.

If the proper setting is established, individuals (groups) will examine their problems.

Any new perceptions resulting from the workshop will cause all past and new experiences to be integrated in a new and different meaning.

IV. Style of Presentation

Informal group discussion.

Direct participation through structured exercises.

V. Materials and Equipment

Films

"Black Anger," Human Development Institute, Inc. Ten- (10) minute film segment of two white employees discussing problems in the plant caused by the hard core.

Slides

Slide presentation illustrating ghetto housing in Rochester. Slides which provide local statistics on nonwhite/white employment/unemployment trends, educational level, types of housing, and so forth.

Other

Instructor and trainee training kits, Human Development Institute, Inc.

Role-play activities.

Two visuals, flannel boards.

VI. The Training Program

1. Session No. 1

A. Trainer Introduction

Explain relationship to NAB training program.

B. Self-Introduction of Participants

Name.

Exhibit 18 (continued)

Department, section, location.
Time with Xerox.
Years as supervisor.

C. <u>Purpose</u> <u>of</u> <u>Workshop</u>
Explain focus of first session of the workshop.

(1) <u>Discussion</u> <u>of</u> <u>Attitudes</u>
White employees' toward the hard core.
Black attitudes about the white man's
world of work.

<u>Purpose</u>
"Within our plant, we experience various
types of behavior which result from the
attitudes and feelings of our existing
workforce and the new hard-core employee.
From this interaction of behaviors, we
sometimes get problems."

"Therefore, we first want to talk about
attitudes because, in order to effectively
deal with problems, we need to get at the
cause."

(2) <u>Discussion</u> <u>of</u> <u>Foremen</u> <u>Feelings</u> <u>and</u> <u>Con-</u>
<u>cerns</u>
Factors which impact on foremen and influence his behavior.

Exhibit 18 (continued)

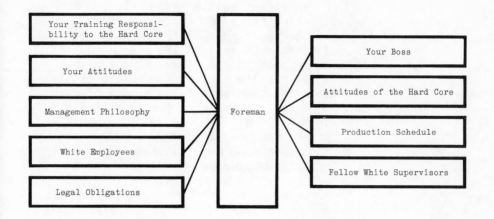

Your Training Responsibility to the Hard Core		Your Boss
Your Attitudes		Attitudes of the Hard Core
Management Philosophy	Foreman	Production Schedule
White Employees		Fellow White Supervisors
Legal Obligations		

<u>Purpose</u>
"To show acceptance and awareness of the various dynamic factors influencing a foreman's role in implementing company policy at the lowest level of operation. To facilitate 'personal-oriented' discussion by recognizing that such factors exist and need discussion."

D. <u>The</u> <u>Program</u>
   (1) <u>Discussion</u> <u>No.</u> <u>1</u>
      Film: two (2) white employees discussing the problems in a plant caused by the hard core.
      <u>Questions</u> <u>Discussed</u> <u>After</u> <u>Viewing</u> <u>the</u> <u>Film</u>
      a. "What were the attitudes and feelings expressed by the two white employees toward the employment of the hard core?"
      b. "I know that some of these same attitudes exist among some of our hourly employees on the floor. How have they expressed their attitudes and feelings? Are they similar or different? If different, how?"

Exhibit 18 (continued)

    c. "What attitudes do you feel were not
       expressed in the film which you know
       exist among our white employees?"

    d. "Recognizing that we are getting hard-
       core employees in the plant and that
       some of the attitudes discussed will
       be prevalent, what are some of the
       steps, you as a foreman, can or have
       taken to deal with these attitudes?"

(2) Discussion No. 2

    Film: "Black Anger."

    "You have seen some attitudes expressed
    by whites toward the hard core in the
    earlier film. Now you will view a film
    expressing the black man's attitudes and
    feelings toward the white man's world of
    work. Remember, they don't necessarily
    represent all blacks or are all hard core,
    but they do describe feelings and atti-
    tudes."

    Questions Discussed After Viewing the Film

    a. "What were the attitudes and feelings
       expressed by the individuals in the
       film toward the white man's world of
       work?"

    b. "I know that some of these same atti-
       tudes exist among some of our black
       employees on the floor. How have they
       expressed their attitudes and feelings?
       Are they similar or different? If dif-
       ferent, how?"

    c. "What attitudes do you feel were not
       expressed in the film which you know
       exist among our black employees?"

    d. "Recognizing that we are getting hard-
       core employees in the plant and that
       some of the attitudes discussed will be
       prevalent, what are some of the steps,
       you as a foreman, can or have taken to
       deal with these attitudes?"

Exhibit 18 (continued)

      (3) <u>Discussion</u> <u>No.</u> 3
         "Are there any general comments about the
         two films?"
      (4) <u>Closing</u> <u>Comments</u>
         Company commitments.
         What the company is doing in terms of
         visible support for foremen.
         Emphasize foreman's role as an instructor.
         "Our next training session will deal more
         directly with some of your problems. In
         addition, we will cover some techniques
         available to uncover the source of the
         problem."

2. <u>Session</u> <u>No.</u> 2
  A. <u>Trainer</u> <u>Introduction</u>
  B. <u>Self-Introduction</u> <u>of</u> <u>Participants</u>
      Name.
      Department, section, location.
      Time with Xerox.
      Years as supervisor.
  C. <u>Introduction—Session</u> <u>No.</u> 2
      (1) <u>Review</u> <u>last</u> <u>Session</u>
         Comment on wall charts of attitudes iden-
         tified from the two films shown during
         the first session.
         "Discussion of attitudes and feelings was
         important because:

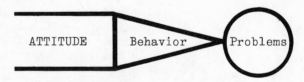

Today, we change the above to:

Exhibit 18 (continued)

"Personal attitudes cause us, in most
cases, to deal with problems at the behavior level.
"There are varied causes to behavior—
some concrete, clear, obvious—some are
vague, dynamic, and multiple.
"Today, our emphasis will be on how you
as foremen can effectively look at a problem, identify and look carefully at behavior in order to determine the cause of
the problem."

TAKE ACTION ON CAUSE NOT JUST BEHAVIOR
D. The Program
    (1) Slide Presentation (Activity No. 1)
        a. "In our last session, we saw blacks and
        whites identify some large-size prob-
        lems. Today, we will view some slides
        which document other problems."
        b. Show slides.
        c. Comment: "The slides do not show
        Newark, Harlem, Watts, or Chicago.
        They show the inner city of Rochester,
        New York. The statistics shown on the
        slides are not national but rather are
        local, Monroe County, Rochester, New
        York."
        d. Comment: "The Xerox commitment in
        Rochester, New York, is in part to
        deal with this paradox—prosperity
        alongside poverty; high employment
        alongside specific kinds of unemploy-
        ment; and quality housing alongside
        poor housing. Xerox is dealing with
        this problem through its job-training
        program, Project Step Up."
    (2) Adjustment to New Situations (Activity
        No. 2)
        a. Introduction:
        "Working with the hard core, it's cru-

Exhibit 18 (continued)

cial to understand the causes of
behavior.
"This exercise will enable you to experience, in part, the feelings a new
hard-core employee may have."
b. <u>Exercise</u>: Developed by the Human Development Institute.
Prism glasses—catch ball, work puzzle.
Foreman complete a check sheet.
Discuss check sheet in terms of the
following factors, which may be part of
a new situation:
1. Adjustment.
2. Embarrassment and anger.
3. Mistrust.
4. Drawn to other new members.
"On the basis of your experience with
the prism glasses, one might safely
assume that the hard core will:
1. "Find it easier going after some
   time has passed.
2. "Be embarrassed and confused since
   they don't know their way around,
   and frustrated when making mistakes.
   Usually this frustration is not
   spoken—it's held in and comes out
   later in different ways. In many
   cases with the hard-core unemployed,
   their response to the frustration
   and confusion they feel at work is
   not to return. Did <u>you</u> have an im-
   pulse to take off the glasses during
   the exercise? All of us stay away
   from unpleasant situations when we
   have a choice. The greatest dropout
   rate in employment programs takes
   place during the first three weeks.
   This has been true in the past because the hard-core unemployed have
   been afraid of failing again, be-

Exhibit 18 (continued)

cause they felt unwelcome, and because they were unsure how to act.
3. "Feel mistrustful. It will take
time for them to build trust with
you. Don't be surprised if they use
that time to test you out and figure
who and what you are. After all—
you will be doing the same things
with them.
4. "Probably stick with others who are
new like them. Don't be surprised if
this happens. Remember how you felt
more comfortable with the other
people wearing glasses. Your new
employees will probably feel more
comfortable with each other."

(3) Awareness of Other Aspects of the New
Hard-Core Employee (Activity No. 3)
a. Introduction
"We have looked closely at the feelings of the hard-core hire on the new
job. In order to understand his behavior, we have to also be aware of
other aspects of the new employee."
(Use Flannel Board)
1. First factory job.
2. Physical limitations.
3. Expecting to fail.
4. Slow reader and learner because of
age or other difficulties.
5. Sensitive.
6. Callous to criticism and resent
authority.
"In addition, remember the hard-core
hire may view you as
1. "The man who may fire him at the
first opportunity.
2. "A man who knows him only as a
number.
3. "A man who doesn't have time to
teach him his job.

Exhibit 18 (concluded)

4. "A man who accepts no explanation
   for lateness, absenteeism, or not
   doing the job right.
5. "A man who always thinks he will
   goof-off.
6. "With suspicion, as you represent
   'authority.' "
   b. Comment
   "This is all key to understanding the
   problem in terms of behavior—cause—
   (Blackboard). We'll now review the
   problem-solving approach for getting
   at some of the causes behind the problem and resolution of such."
   (4) Problem Solving (Activity No. 4)
   a. Review all four steps.
   Gather information.
   State the problem.
   Consider the alternative.
   Commit to action.
   b. Provide role-play activities dealing
   with problems experienced by the hard
   core and foremen. Foremen deal with
   these problems by using the four steps
   to problem solving.
   (5) Closing Discussion
   This is an unstructured activity in which
   we provide an opportunity for foremen to
   discuss any specific concerns, unanswered
   questions, and personally experienced
   problems.

6. On the Job: Supervision, Counseling, Supportive Services

GENERAL MOTORS CORPORATION hired more than 21,705 hard-core unemployed in its plants around the country between April 1 and November 30, 1968, according to *The Wall Street Journal*. James M. Roche, chairman, said that last April the company told the National Alliance of Businessmen it would hire about 12,759 perennially unemployed by June 30, 1969.

"It now seems certain that the original projections will be more than doubled before that date," Mr. Roche said. For that period of eight months "the hard core constituted 20 percent of those added to employee rolls. Of the 21,705 hired, 54 percent were nonwhite, 46 percent were white. The retention rate of the hard-core employee is 67.6 percent while for all other workers hired during the same period the retention rate is 67.9 percent."[1]

A large California aerospace company says the retention rate of hard-core unemployed has been better than that for highly skilled workers and, "There's real company loyalty among them."[2]

To achieve such loyalty, companies must be aware that the unemployed hard core are seeking meaningful jobs. Richard Ford, of the Nassau County, N.Y., Economic Opportunity Commission, says: "Some businessmen think that there are a lot of mythical characters called [hard core] running around looking for jobs that pay $1.60 or $1.70 an hour. They're sadly mistaken. Minimum-wage jobs hold little appeal for many reasons. Transportation to and from work alone takes up a good part of a minimum wage. In the case of work-

---

[1] *The Wall Street Journal,* January 7, 1969.
[2] *American Machinist,* June 3, 1968.

ing mothers who may also be heads of households, the problem of child care adds to the problem."[3]

Welfare recipients often express the opinion that minimum wages would leave them worse off than if they remained on welfare. Many claim they would prefer to work, but can't afford to at the wages offered. One of the keys to retention is a meaningful job at a reasonable wage.

THE SUPERVISOR IS THE KEY MAN

Early in the employment period tardiness or excessive absenteeism might be a warning signal. Leon Woods, general manager of Watts Manufacturing Company, a subsidiary formed by Aerojet General Corporation, faced this problem and solved it in a unique way: "We just sent for them. We put some workers in cars and had them go and bring the others in. Later we devised a buddy system where a worker with some time on the job would assume responsibility for a new hire, and part of that responsibility was to get him to work on time. Before long that person is on his own and is ready to help someone else."

In the Los Angeles area an employer was confronted with the problem of lateness but rarely absenteeism. Investigation revealed that the new hires lacked the money needed for alarm clocks and were oversleeping. A director of training suggested this approach, "Think positively; assume that lateness or absenteeism is being caused by something beyond the trainee's control. Then approach the problem with an attitude of helping to solve a problem. This permits you and the trainee to dig out the causes. The opposite approach may blind you to the reasons because they may not seem rational to you on the basis of your experiences."

It has also been widely reported that some hard-core employees were not able to get to their jobs because they could not read the bus markings. This was particularly true in the Detroit area. Sometimes the new employee makes it to work, but is not in a position to perform his duties. As one executive recalled:

---

[3] *Ibid.*

If a guy comes in drunk—and there was a lot of this on Monday mornings—we tend to send him home. We tell him to come back when he's sobered up. That's made a difference in our program. In effect, we're saying to him, "We want you." And we demonstrate it. We know that on Monday mornings there is a high absenteeism rate. We sometimes ran as high as 50 percent. That's a costly process. So we started with the good workers. If we knew where they were we sent somebody out to bring them in. "We need you, man." Boy, that's a pretty strong message. And pretty soon it becomes believable. . . . The guy who is the real hard core has never really been wanted. Nobody ever *wanted* that man before.

The National Alliance of Businessmen advises in its "Guidelines for Introducing the Hard-Core Unemployed to a Productive Job" that disciplinary rules may have to be modified during the early stages of employment. Many hard core have never lived by the clock.

"Then, too," the booklet states, "the employee-trainee will have certain character traits acquired over the years of frustration or boredom." Here are some items that are based on actual cases of adjustments reported by the NAB:

- Many Negroes from poor neighborhoods believe a "hat" is a sign of manhood and should be worn at all times. . . .
- To the disadvantaged, music [transistor radio] has often been a substitute for conversation.
- Hard-core unemployed workers have experienced complete disorientation when hit with the factory noises of heavy industry.
- The hard core respond well to simple rules that are backed up with authority and immediate action if the rule is broken.

In addition, according to NAB, "The hard-core employee, emerging from an environment where there are no fixed routines and exposed to the culture shock [of working for the first time with a majority of white employees] will be ill-disposed toward discipline in the early stages of his training. . . . Existing standards with regard to such items as fighting, theft, or gambling should probably be equitably enforced without separate treatment for the hard core. Such items as tardiness and absenteeism may require modification for the hard core during a longer probationary period."

These thoughts were supported by experiences with the hard core that were discussed by a manufacturing executive. He pointed out: "Many of the trainees exhibit status aspirations far above their indicated ability, making the holding down of an entry-level job, considered honorable and acceptable to others, as no more than a flunky position in their eyes. This is further compounded by an almost hysterical distaste for appearing what in their eyes they assume to be an Uncle Tom."

Often, to thwart any appearance of being an Uncle Tom, a hard-core employee will demonstrate unusual aggressiveness. While order taking is an accepted notion for most workers, the hard core see this as a sign of inferiority and, therefore, often resent being "told what to do" by a supervisor.

Furthermore, many hard-core workers are simply not impressed by "authority" or "hierarchy of management," so the simple task of giving orders in the work situation becomes somewhat complex when the orders are issued to the newly employed man from the streets. As one executive recalled:

> It seems to me that one of the things we have learned is that each supervisor must give more detailed supervision. He has got to guide, lead, counsel as well as direct. We have to continually emphasize communication.
>
> We found that you have got to repeat and repeat. You've got to make sure it got heard. Repeat it until it's really clarified. I think that this whole business of seeking feedback, to find out if he really understands you, is one of the important keys.
>
> We found that with the hard-core group, if you say, "Do something," and he is a new employee, he'll say, "Yes, sir," and then go do what he wants to do. Now there are many reasons for this. First of all he either doesn't understand authority, or he is unimpressed, or he is rebelling against authority.
>
> When we think in terms of his point of reference, authority to him has meant the police department, sometimes the department of welfare, or the gang leaders, or a bully. What picture is conjured up in this man's mind when you say, "Do such and such"?

In this company the supervisors try to teach the hard core that there is a procedure for everything they do. If there is no procedure, the work will wait, unless it absolutely has to be done, until a procedure can be developed. The constant attempt to impress the hard-core workers that the business world is run on procedures lessens the onus of the authority issue, and a smoother work flow results.

In another company an executive commented:

> They don't know our language. They will say, "I understand," with that dull look in the eye, and make mistake after mistake. Everything has to be explained at least five times and then demonstrated. You begin by saying, "This is a socket wrench." Few of them have ever seen tools or know how to use them. The first three days are totally lost. They distrust everything they are told. They never ask questions or admit mistakes. They are too insecure.

In this company it was discovered that some rough spots had to be smoothed during the early days of employment when the first hard-core trainees were assigned to regular jobs. The foremen originally thought that they should "treat everybody the same." They were not made aware that the hard core would require much more attention. For example, as soon as tardiness or absenteeism began to develop, the foremen would tend to let it build up and then present the record as "Exhibit A" in trying to convince the personnel and training departments (whose consent was needed) to fire the hard core who weren't shaping up. The company approached this problem by assigning specific counselors to visit with the hard-core employees each day of their on-the-job experience to try to nip potential problems before they would occur.

But sometimes the situations the supervisor may have to deal with on the job will test the best of his abilities. The supervisor must be skilled in dealing with a unique social situation. For example, one executive recounted:

> The supervisor suspected that one of his people was "high." But you can't really tell. It's difficult to tell even if you know someone well. You just don't know whether they are on the stuff or not. Their behavior is erratic.

Now in the white industrial world the supervisor would go to him and pull him out and send him to sick bay for the doctor to examine. If he was on the stuff he would be fired. That's the way it works.

But our role is not to fire him. Our job is to keep him employed. So what do we do? Here's how this supervisor handled it. He knew this guy had a friend, an old-time employee of the company. The supervisor went to the man's friend and said, "It looks to me" —notice he did not accuse the guy, he did not say he is on the stuff. He said, "It looks to me like he might be on the stuff."

He did not condemn the guy. He gave him and his friend the opportunity to save face. He said, "I don't want to talk to him now because I may find out he is, but I want you to go to him and talk to him. Now if he is, get him out of here, get him home and tell him he is not to come back until he is off it."

This is a different way. What good did it do? Well, the guy came back to work and he was off the stuff. Then the supervisor talked to him to the effect that, "We need you to work with us; it's important, but if you're on the stuff you can be a danger to yourself and to the other guys. We can't have it. We understand the problem, but we can't have it while you work."

That incident happened months ago, and as far as we can tell the man has not come in again in that condition. It could be that this guy is saved, rehabilitated. And the guy is a good worker; he was a good worker at the time. This is one of those situations where a supervisor did a pretty good job, in my estimation, of playing it by ear. He was not told to do this.

A much stronger emphasis on immediate discipline was evident in another firm. This company believed that any problem that is not stopped as soon as it is discovered builds destructive momentum. Furthermore, this company had read about the permissive "coddling" of the hard core in some other companies and found such permissiveness quite alien to its own temperament. This kind of strong approach, it was felt, did not make the hard core feel like social cripples. The approach was intended to make them feel useful and help them cope with their problems as equals to those problems, erasing as well any "welfare mentality" that might have been in the backs of their minds.

It must be remembered that in this company's program far too many of these youths had become "agency babies," a situation into which they had been pushed and prodded but never truly allowed to act and deal with the consequences of their acts with proper guidance and support. Although it was not unusual for them to get slapped for their acts, information about why they had been slapped had seldom been given or incorporated into the minds of these youths, except as dismissal and rejection. In short, by the hard core's being aware of these problems, the supervisors expected them to make it on the job; and, consequently, this expectation helped them feel capable of making it.

The supervisor also has to deal with the way that other workers view the hard core. The initial training group in another company was almost immediately identified as "The Untouchables" or "The Raiders," and the other workers felt that the hard core were the plant "babies," who received special treatment. And indeed they were. This characterization contributed to some tension and misunderstanding, especially when the trainees who exhibited little desire to work, and showed poor attitude, were allowed to "get away with it" for awhile in the program's attempt to assimilate them into the workforce.

It soon became somewhat obvious to the supervisors that hard-core workers who exhibited the worst of unacceptable behavior and work habits (such as going to sleep under a pile of stacked material) showed little if any improvement unless reasonably stringent standards were laid down and enforced, and the requirement that they be adhered to clearly stated, with termination from the program resulting where response was negative.

The "alienness" of the trainee works against him. All those features that are common, or dismissed if not accepted, in the ghetto stamp the trainee as an outsider in the work situation. Considering the great many things working against the trainee—poor skill, poor attitudes, poor behavior, and racial discrimination—dealing with the building up of a new and more acceptable "image" is common sense, even an indispensable part of the supervisor's job in working toward helping the trainees. Chances are that any supervisor unfamiliar with ghettoized youth who perceives the standards of appearance and behavior in essentially middle-class terms would be frightened and sometimes shocked and repelled in his first contact with some of these young people.

Counseling and Supportive Services Are Required

Counseling and supportive services are key elements in the structure of planning that helps the hard-core worker adjust to the work situation and to regular schedules. The support given to the hard-core trainee varies from firm to firm, depending largely upon the company, its size, location, the number of hard core involved, and the economic considerations.

The first task of any counseling effort is to define and understand the goals to be achieved. In order to be effective, a counselor must be aware of trainee interests, problems, aims, and needs. A close working relationship will do much to guarantee the success of the trainee. The adviser must also make himself available to the trainee. The ultimate aim of all counselors is to be of help to the individual.

"It's touchy in the early stages," a bank personnel manager said. "You try to sound friendly, but you can easily edge over into paternalism. That they resent."

The counselors who seem to have achieved success apparently have a strong and mature ego. They have an empathetic understanding of others. They have found it vital to keep the revelations of the trainees in the strictest confidence. They have learned to be shock-proof to the revelations that might be made to them by trainees. Many of the things they hear may be foreign to their own behavior.

A counselor has eliminated, as much as one can, his biases concerning race, color, creed, and any other values that he may hold. The counselor must win the confidence of the trainee and set the tone for interchange. Honesty is the basis of confidence. Above all else, the counselor exercises complete candor with the trainees. Nothing will destroy the relationship quicker than any evidence, however slim, that the counselor is being dishonest.

It is wise for a counselor not to push for rapport more quickly than will be acceptable to the trainee. Trainees will question his motives if he attempts to get "buddy-buddy" too quickly. An easy pace works best.

Perhaps the best-known and most widely used support is the "buddy system," which pairs mature, sympathetic workers with new hires on a one-to-one basis. This allows the new hires to have a source of information. Many of the hard core use these "buddies" for on-the-job help as well as a source of understanding and reassurance. In many instances the new hire confides in his "buddy" matters of a personal nature. The key to success for such an approach is that the senior "buddy" is sincere in his desire to aid the disadvantaged worker to make it on the job.

The "job coach," not new to industry but playing a new role, is a support used by many companies. Job coaches in the past usually demonstrated the way they wanted something done and then permitted the trainee to try. They would correct errors and after a few tries could move on to something else. With the hard core the job coach's job is more difficult.

Philco-Ford found in its training center in Philadelphia that many of the hard core were not acquainted with many of the tools commonly used in machine shops. An even more difficult hurdle was the time it took for the trainee to gain confidence in his ability to operate a piece of machinery. A good job coach can build into a person the confidence needed to stay on the job. The job coach must above all else have the ingredients that make a good teacher. He, too, like the "buddy," must have the desire and patience needed to participate in such an arrangement. Successful job coaches must keep pretty close to the trainee and have the capacity to win his confidence. In all probability, he may also be drawn into the personal affairs of the trainee and his family.

I believe that most workers can be helped to make it into the economic mainstream with either the buddy system or the job coach approach. It is found that work, plus the confidence one gains from being able to produce, is beneficial therapy. The hard core quickly learn to relate in a positive manner to their work and their co-workers.

However, some hard core may require professional attention if they are to ever become productive employees. Only one of the companies surveyed had undertaken this task. It is a job that requires a professionally trained person. It is not a task for the buddy or the job coach to tackle. At Lockheed-Georgia, a technique known as psychodrama was employed. Psychodrama is a tool used to allow the participants to role play in such a way that they are able to gain insight into some of their own attitudes and some of the attitudes of the people with whom they will come into contact. The sessions are unstructured and can lead almost anywhere.

The session that I attended had a trainee playing the role of a personnel officer interviewing one other trainee for a job. The leader had the task of setting the scene and then keeping it moving. The pace is stepped up and fast moving, apparently to elicit responses that are not planned or thought out and in this way attempt to get at some of the real feeling that the trainees otherwise might not express. If the session or role playing lags, the leader enters and attempts by questions to keep it going. When the session reaches its conclusion, the other 13 trainees, who served as an audience, criticize the exercise and try to draw out things they think the trainees did wrong. The setting provided an opportunity for trainees who had problems to share their feelings in a nonthreatening setting. They were being encouraged to face their fears and conflicts and, it was hoped, would be freed from some of the inner pressures that prohibited them from coping with the world of work. The leader was also available to the trainees after these sessions, and they seemed to make use of the opportunity to talk with him to clear up some of their misconceptions and thus function better.

Some companies may be tempted to employ the use of professional psychologists for all the hard-core trainees, on the assumption that they all need extraordinary help. This is surely one way to drive the hard core out of the plant. The majority do not need it. Most companies avoid going this extra mile in attempting to recoup individuals who need professional help. In the interview they seek to screen out the very serious cases. Cases of this type were seldom reported by companies, so they are perhaps rare.

In addition to these counseling efforts, which are part of the working environment, companies are offering other supportive services to help the hard core deal with their off-the-job problems.

Most people, at one time or another, have had to unsnarl the financial knot that can play havoc with one's income. Poor people for many reasons are more prone to the snare. Many companies, Economic Systems Corporation, Boston, being one of them, provide employees information on credit buying and legal matters and help educate them as consumers. In some instances, outside experts are brought in to discuss their particular fields. The Legal Aid Society is often asked to inform the new hires of the availability of legal service in the event that they need legal help.

The major reason many women quit work or are frequently absent or late is the child-care problem. Working mothers must seek out suitable persons to care for their children while they work. They often use relatives, friends, and neighbors on a paid or unpaid basis. In some instances settlement houses, nurseries, and private day-care centers are used. In the event of any breakdown in these arrangements, the mother is forced to be late or to stay home. Companies may find that they may soon become directly involved in day-care centers —if only to keep competent workers from having to leave the job.

The National Association of Manufacturers reports that the KLH Research and Development Corporation also provides day-care centers for children whose mothers must work. The center has been located near the factory, and the mother pays a small weekly tuition fee. What is unique about the KLH center is that it goes beyond the usual concept of merely keeping the children occupied. In fact, the center is a school with a professional staff of teachers and aides.

The National Alliance of Businessmen suggests in its booklet that "factors which constitute the hard core's existence—poverty, lack of education, insecurity, poor diet, bad housing, and the like—will make life difficult during his first months on the job. Problems that would appear trifling to most employees may seem insurmountable to the recruits." NAB advises that the types of extraordinary supportive services they may be necessary are

- Medical and dental services.
- Legal aid.
- Day care services.
- Transportation.
- Personal budgeting and financial service.

Financial support includes education in handling wages, making the money last to next payday, the use of insurance, income tax and withholding tax, employee benefits, use of banking services, guidelines on obtaining loans and avoiding unscrupulous credit practices, and also the community agencies that can help. NAB advises that all hard-core employees can be bonded, if a company desires, by the State Employment Service.

The author has observed that in some cases it may be necessary to make small loans to the hard-core worker every day until he has learned to budget and plan ahead.

Companies are not in agreement as to how far they should go to try to catch the hard-core worker each time he trips. Some counsel against coddling, making them too dependent. Others believe that these employees grow out of dependence to self-assurance and independence. What one company may view as overconcern another considers a necessary show of interest. There is some consensus, however, that if the company, as exemplified by the staff and other employees with whom the hard core have contact, feels real concern, that feeling will be communicated. The essentially fearful, somewhat distrustful, often angry new worker from the ghetto will begin to sense that the company actually means to help him.

If the climate of the company is essentially accepting and warm, most hard-core people will be motivated to respond in a positive manner. This is a basic step in the process of effectively retaining the hard core.

Some supportive programs are now designed to provide positive gains for the regular workforce as well as the hard core. As one personnel director put it, "We have backed into a new managerial technique." He explains it this way:

> We found that a smaller percentage of hard-core trainees were leaving their jobs than were newly hired nondisadvantaged white workers. So we came to the conclusion that the extra attention provided by staff, along with special support services, would be good for *all* employees, not just the hard core.

> Toward this end, our staff has become increasingly attuned to approaching each employee on an individual basis, in terms of his particular strengths and limitations. We believe that because we are now responsive to the worker's needs, the company has cut down on job dropouts, across the board.

The Prospect of Mobility Is Essential

The hard core, as this report stresses, have tasted failure too often. They need not only to experience success but also to be assured that the company appreciates their achievements and gives them concrete recognition. For the chronically unemployed person to stay with a job long enough to become a respected member of the regular labor force *is* an achievement.

Pay increases and further skill acquisition leading to eventual promotion are generally the rewards for tenure and achievement. But one company that established a hard-core operation in the slums decided to add something extra. After six months of satisfactory performance on the job, a worker receives a written commendation. At the end of the first year, he receives a special pin. Men who are trained to be supervisors get a certificate after successful completion of their training. In the overall picture, such rewards may not seem important. But the advice is not to sell this concept short. Middle-class whites may joke about a pin or a gold watch received from an employer, but underneath the levity there is often a feeling of a closer bond with the company, which is no longer seen as quite so impersonal. Some imaginative form of tangible reward for achievement may help the disadvantaged worker to develop a feeling that he belongs.

An increasing number of companies involved in hard-core programs have concluded that hiring and training are only the first steps in the process of effectively employing the disadvantaged. If these employees are to feel they have any real future in the organization, job tenure must be a reality for them. They need to know that good work performance can lead to higher wages and greater job security. Some companies, however, have focused so exclusively on the hiring and training process that they have given little thought to the retention question. IBM, Pacific Tel. & Tel., and others that participated in the interviews are examples of companies that already have programs to assist these new employees to increase their skills and move ahead in the organization. As one executive put it, "This not only provides us with needed skilled workers but also opens up entry-level jobs for other unemployed people."

A number of systematic approaches are being used to encourage upward mobility. One is the open-job posting system; AVCO Corporation's subsidiary in Roxbury, Massachusetts, posts all job openings and the requirements in an accessible location. This has the twofold effect of enabling those who feel they meet the qualifications to bid on the job and of letting others who do not have the qualifications see what they must do to prepare themselves for future openings.

While posting unquestionably increases upward mobility and en-

courages employees to learn new skills, it also requires real commitment on the part of the company if it is to work. For instance, it is
essential to explain fully to those who apply but do not get a job why
they were passed over and suggest how they may improve their chances
for promotion in the future. Whether the investment required to establish and maintain a posting system is seen as worthwhile obviously
depends on the individual company. But there is general agreement
that companies involved with the hard core should develop methods
that will encourage employees to more fully realize their potentialities
in the work setting. For employees with drive and ability, dead-end
jobs engender only frustration and despair and result in high turn-
over, absenteeism, and lateness. This sense of frustration was recently
expressed by a hard-core worker in a large plant:

> If Whitey thinks it's enough to get me in a job, to get me to work
> every day, I've got news—it's not enough. If I'm not accomplish-
> ing anything, if I'm not getting anywhere, it's the same as welfare.
> Unless "the man" can make me feel I'm doing something and go-
> ing somewhere—that I'm part of something real—he can forget
> his job.

Staff people involved in efforts to employ the hard core through
community programs sponsored by public or nonprofit private agencies have had difficulty keeping adequate day-by-day records of what
happens to the trainees. The importance of disciplined record keeping
seems to have gotten lost in the excitement. As a result, valuable data
that could have pointed up lessons for the future were sometimes not
recorded.

To resolve problems of this kind, one personnel director, responsible for his company's hard-core program, pointed out that his staff
is keeping a "diary," in which all pertinent details and events are
noted for future reference. The program is far enough along for him
to realize that an incredible number of "happenings" occur daily,
which are enlightening as well as challenging. He feels the diary will
serve a variety of purposes, from having public relations value to helping to chart a more fruitful long-range program. By setting up a system for documentation of facts and figures, staff with the necessary
expertise can make a valuable contribution to additional research and
sharing of information.

EXHIBIT 19. *Evaluation of One of the Hard-Core Training Groups at the Rochester Facility of Xerox Corporation*

Trainee No.	Weeks in Program	Hours in Basic Education	Activities	Rating	Comments
1	4	28.5	See attached	Satisfactory	Good attitude; could progress more rapidly if he had more ambition.
2	4	24.0	"	Satisfactory	Hindered somewhat by absence. Works well, but occasionally displays impatience with others.
3	4	28.5	"	Satisfactory	Excellent oral vocabulary, but doesn't recognize written words. Keen perception shown in discussions. Could do more independent work.
4	4	22.5	"	Satisfactory	Works well; good attitude, but hindered by frequent absence.
5	4	21.0	"	Satisfactory	Good attitude, hindered by absence. Excellent contributions in discussions.
6	4	30.0	"	Good	Works very well independently—shows definite improvement.
7	4	31.5	"	Good	Excellent attitude; works very well—reads independently.
8	4	31.5	"	Satisfactory	Quick wit—shows good perception in discussions. A "nervous" test taker.
9	4	31.5	"	Satisfactory	Very quiet, but shows good attitude.

Exhibit 19 (concluded)

10	4	31.5	"	Good	Works well; excellent attitude. Shows some improvement.
11	4	28.5	"	Satisfactory	Works rapidly with fair efficiency. "Covers" mistakes rather than getting them squared away.
12	4	28.5	"	Fair	Very good attitude, but definitely slow. Farthest apart from the group in terms of achievement.
13	2	16.5	"	Good	Follows with lip reading amazingly well. A very good and an industrious worker.
14	2	15.0	"	Good	Quiet, but works well. Good attitude.

EXHIBIT 20. *An Informal Summary of the Effects of Motivating and Counseling on the Lockheed Hard-Core Program; Prepared by the Education and Training Department*

16 May 1968

TRAINING THE HARD-CORE UNEMPLOYED— MOTIVATING AND COUNSELING

The following has been taken from an informal report on training the hard-core unemployed. The items listed deal with the motivating and counseling aspects of LMSC's program.

1. I think the biggest factor we had going for us in our program was the fact that a man started drawing a *good* wage as soon as he came into the program. There are two reasons why this is important:
   A. More than one man who had been receiving welfare aid told us ours was the only training he could afford to take; that is, the equivalent of unemployment insurance for the duration of the training program under the usual MDTA effort just couldn't match the welfare money he had been getting, while our $2.68 per hour, plus the 19¢ COL, could.

Exhibit 20 (continued)

    B. These people are not long-term-goal-oriented. They had a job *now,* not "maybe," or not "X" months down the road if they completed their training. I'm sure this is one of the big items which held our turnover during training to almost zero. Incidentally, we did lose one well-endowed lass to San Francisco's tenderloin district. Redmon just didn't have enough money in his merit fund to enable us to make her rate competitive with the take from the "oldest profession."

2. The men were trained for good jobs—jobs they could go out into their neighborhood and talk about. These weren't the traditional janitor jobs; they were jobs that called for the mastery of skills.

3. We stayed away from the classroom atmosphere. These men were school dropouts; it wouldn't have been smart to take them back into a failure atmosphere. The training was for real; it was highly job-related.

4. Classes were small; the men could receive a lot of needed individual attention. There were no long, frustrating waits for information.

5. The instructors were tops. Not only did they know the work, but they were interested in what they were doing; this was more than just another assignment to them.

6. Because the classes were small and the instructors were interested in really helping the trainees, it was possible to quickly establish some real rapport with them. When a man had a personal problem, he wasn't sent off to see some "head candler" whom he saw only when he was in trouble; he talked to the instructor.

7. When a man did need help, he got action quickly. If this meant towing his car off a freeway, we did it. If he had to go to jail, someone out of the training department whom he knew was down there with him to talk to the judge to see what could be done to fix things. In one instance, for example, we worked it out, so that the man could continue with his training while he spent his nights and weekends in jail until he had served out his sentence. News of this kind of help gets around. You would be surprised how many people have dropped off a card to Stan Hawkins, supervisor of the program, thanking him for all the help he gave them.

8. The training was conducted right here in the training building, where employees are continually coming and going at all hours, taking classes to improve their capability. Our VIP'ers had a chance to see other members of their minority group taking these classes; thus they were, in at least one sense, part of the mainstream already.

Exhibit 20 (continued)

9. The training atmosphere was businesslike, and it certainly was friendly also. More than one graduating class brought in a cake and invited their instructor and a few of the rest of us to share it.

10. We made it a point to bring in the supervisor to meet the trainee he would eventually get upon completion of the training. And before graduation, the trainee was taken out to the area where he was to work. The supervisor did more than shake hands with his man; he was provided with the opportunity to talk with him to explain the nature of the work he'd be doing.

11. There was OJT follow-up on the part of the instructor. After his man went onto the job, the instructor was expected to maintain regular and frequent contact with the new man. In some cases, this is where some of the most meaningful help was given. Personal problems arose long after the man had left the formal training program. The men continued to turn to the instructor, whom they had learned to trust. As a matter of fact, this was a problem we had; we wanted people to realize that the VIP program was not just a program which Education and Training was running; it was everyone's program. We wanted the personnel representatives, the supervisors, the employee service people—everyone to have a strong desire to make the program a success. At times we felt others were too inclined to refer to the newly assigned workers, when talking to us, as "your VIP'ers" or "your hard-core people."

12. Six months after the trainees had been on the job we planned to give them some more training to a maximum of 50 hours. The purpose of this additional training was to strengthen skills in which they had already been trained and to give them new skills so they could have a better chance for upgrading. We felt the upgrading factor would be particularly important, for we did not want to have these men stuck in entry-level jobs. We wanted to get as many as we could away from the situation of "last hired–first fired" which so often prevails with unskilled employees. We did not carry through with this part of the program. We got rumbles of complaint from other employees, who wanted equal training opportunities; the union brought up the question also, so we eased off on this effort. We decided, rather, upon a soft sell of training after hours on a voluntary basis.

13. Although a concerted counseling effort is just getting under way, and while admittedly we're comparing fewer than a hundred VIP'ers with close to 10,000 technical people, we now have a higher percentage of

Exhibit 20 (continued)

our hard-core people taking courses on their own time than we have engineers and scientists doing so. Fortunately, there have been openings in the higher job classifications, and a number of our VIP'ers have been able to qualify for them by taking some prescribed courses. Again, this word gets around. Poor people can get used to the idea of having more money, too, and we've found that a great many can be motivated to take the training that will enable them to get it.

14. We made provisions this year to bring in professional social workers on a scheduled basis. We found we could handle the in-plant problems, but working on the trainees' family problems, too, would be too much for us if we had 200 trainees. We have set up an office for the social workers, replete with phone, typewriter, and so on. We haven't started our VIP program yet this year, so we have no comments about the effectiveness of this approach; there is no doubt in my mind, however, that it will prove to be a valuable one.

15. We are making it a point to be concerned about our VIP'ers even after layoff. We give them a small booklet when we discuss their being laid off. We also supply them with a résumé, which they take along with them when applying for a job at another company. We actively try to get jobs for our people with local companies, and we do everything we can to make them feel they are *our* people, people in whom we have a real investment, people we want back. Further, we want them to feel they have a skill now, something which they can sell at a good price. I think they are finding this out, for so far, since the first of the year, 12 of our VIP'ers have been laid off. Nine have found other jobs in local companies (one has left the area, another has failed to report for three interviews, a third says she wants to work only for Lockheed and has enough money to last until such time as she thinks she will be recalled to her old job). Incidentally, we are doing everything we can to get our people placed. Two individuals, for example, are even now receiving special training in microwelding at company expense. We had surplused them; Philco said they would hire them except for the fact that they didn't know how to do microwelding. I might not be able to do it every time, but right now I can spare the instructor to do the training (about 40 hours) and we are doing it.

I guess in final analysis, when you talk about motivating and counseling these people, you get off to an awfully good start if you just treat them like human beings. A little patience and understanding can do a lot to make a program such as ours succeed.

EXHIBIT 21. *Ford Motor Company's Detroit Recruiting Project—Analysis of Hires; Prepared by Ford*

Detroit Recruiting Project–Analysis of Hires

An analysis of the first 1,200 hires under the Detroit Recruiting Project and a second group of 1,100 hires revealed the following information:

Retention Rate

Employees in the first group had a retention rate of 78 percent; this figure is based on an average of two months' employment. The rate for the second group surveyed at the point where they had similar service was 79 percent. This compares with a retention rate of 71 percent for other employees with similar service.

Reasons for Termination for Second Group

Type of Termination	Percent of Total
Quit	36.4
Discharge	60.5
Other	3.1
Total	100.0

The reasons for the quits for second group were as follows:

	Percent		Percent
Job Too Hard or Dissatisfied	25.6	Does Not Like Shift	2.4
Leaving Town	6.1	Family Difficulties	1.2
Another Job or Recalled to Former Job	4.9	Transportation Difficulties	1.2
Personal Illness	2.4	Stopped Reporting for Work–Reasons	
Returning to School	2.4	Unknown	53.8
		Total	100.0

Exhibit 21 (continued)

The reasons for the discharges for second group are listed below:

	Percent		Percent
Absenteeism	67.7	Intoxication	0.7
Tardiness	8.1	Refused Job	0.7
Falsified Records	2.2	Miscellaneous	
Disrespect to		Reasons	19.1
Authority	1.5		
		Total	100.0

Absenteeism was, by far, the chief cause of discharge for both groups, constituting about 60 percent of the discharges for the first group and 67.7 percent of such terminations among the second group surveyed.

Supervisory Evaluations

The line supervisor's job performance ratings of the active employees in two TAAP groups as of the date of the survey were as follows:

	First Group Surveyed	Second Group Surveyed
Above Average	35%	20%
Average	47	43
Below Average	18	37
	100%	100%

While the quality of the second group studied has slipped somewhat from that of the first group, it still appears significant that 63 percent were rated average or above by their supervisors.

Age

The TAAP accessions disclosed an average age of slightly more than two years' higher service than the average age of active hourly workers with similar service at the end of 1967.

Absenteeism

The absence rate of both groups of TAAP hires was compared with the absence rate of all employees in the company with comparable age and service. This comparison showed that absenteeism for the TAAP groups was slightly higher than for other employees.

Exhibit 21 (concluded)

Education

The average education of the TAAP hires showed the following comparison with a random group of nonwhites:

| | Random Group 230 Nonwhites | TAAP Accessions | |
		Initial Group	Second Group
Average Education	10.8 years	10.3 years	10.3 years
Percent 0–8 Grade	5%	17%	18%
Percent 9–11 Grade	50	60	55
Percent High School Graduate	45	23	27

Employment Status at Time of Hire

The incidence of unemployment and the length of unemployment prior to hire by the Company was found to be quite similar for both groups surveyed.

	Initial Group	Second Group
Percent Unemployed When Hired	73	70
Percent Unemployed for Designated Periods		
6 months or more	33	31
3 to 6 months	20	25
Less than 3 months	47	44

The fact that approximately 70 percent were unemployed at time of hire and about 75 percent were high school dropouts tends to confirm the fact that we have been recruiting from among the hard-core unemployed.

EXHIBIT 22. *Outline of Xerox Corporation Orientation on Promotion and Transfer*

INDUSTRIAL ORIENTATION
PROMOTION AND TRANSFER

```
 I.  Who am I? What does my job include?
II.  Contract definition—3 levels available
     A. Entry—labor grade 3
     B. Labor pool—labor grade 4, 5, 6
     C. Base jobs
```

Exhibit 22 (continued)

      B. Labor pool—labor grade 4, 5, 6

      C. Base jobs

      D. MD seniority

      E. Labor pool seniority

      F. Job seniority

III.   Transfers

      A. No lateral transfers in entry level

      B. One preferential lateral transfer in labor pool

      C. Transfers within and between job classifications

      D. Six-month restriction on voluntary transfer
         between BP/SD/M and ISD

IV. Promotions

      A. Entry job to labor pool

         1. MD seniority

         2. Qualifications

      B. Labor pool to base jobs

         1. Labor pool seniority

         2. Qualifications of training/experience

      C. Above base jobs

         1. Job seniority

         2. Qualifications of training and/or experi-
            ence

V.   General areas of progression

      A. Stock handling

      B. Quality control

      C. Assembly

      D. Finishing

      E. Manufacturing

      F. Sheet metal

      G. Toolroom

      H. Model shop

VI. Qualifications

      A. Entry level to labor pool
         —completion of E.A.S.

      B. Labor pool to base job
         —Xerox blueprint reading

      C. Above base job
         —completion of course requirements and/or
         experience

VII. Stock handling

      A. Crater-Packer (U-1)

         1. Six months as U-6

         2. Promote to nothing

      B. Tool Crib Attendant (J-25)

Exhibit 22 (concluded)

               1. Promote to Air Tool Repairman and Crib
                  Attendant (J-27)
          C. Receiving and Shipping Clerk (Q-1)
               1. Promote to nothing
          D. Fork Lift Truck Driver (H-8)
               1. Xerox fork lift training
               2. Promote to
                  a. Outside truck (M-4)
                  b. Employment chauffeur (M-7)
VIII. Quality Control
          A. Inspector III (V-8, V-12)
               1. Promote to Inspector I
          B. Tester II (V-10, V-14, V-16)
               1. Promote to Tester I (V-9, V-13, V-15)
  IX. Assembly
          A. Electrical Assembler II (S-7, S-22)
               1. Promote to Electrical Assembler I (S-5,
                  S-14, S-21)
          B. Mechanical Assembler II (S-3, S-13, S-18)
               1. Promote to Mechanical Assembler I (S-2,
                  S-17, S-24)
   X. Finishing
          A. Plater (T-5)
               1. Nine months' experience as T-4 or verifi-
                  able experience
               2. Promote to Solution Maintenance Operator
                  (T-6)
          B. Painter II (T-3)
               1. Six months' experience as T-4 or verifi-
                  able experience
               2. Promote to Painter I (T-2)
  XI. Machining
          A. Auxiliary Machine Operator (R-18)
               1. Xerox Machine Training I or verifiable
                  experience
               2. Promote to Table-Drill Operator (R-17)

  XII. Sheet Metal
          A. Punch-Press Operator II (P-5)
               1. Promote to
                  a. Resistance Welding (P-10)
                  b. Shear Operator (P-6)

EXHIBIT 23. *"Language of the Indigenous"; an Excerpt from the Curriculum Outline for Training the Hard Core at Economic Systems Corporation, Roxbury Plant, Division of AVCO*

LANGUAGE OF THE INDIGENOUS

There is no set language that will remain constant in a universal way in a world of change. Different groups in various geographic locations add, modify, or delete as events, conditions, and personalities indicate change is needed. The following compilation of terms or expressions is not typical of any one group, but is an attempt to gather the "language" of many diverse contemporary groups into one effort. It should serve to introduce persons new to a close proximity with the indigenous to an understanding of what might otherwise sound like a foreign language. In addition to the indigenous, the "hippie" vocabulary is included. There is no typical group that the "language" is derived from, but Negro, Spanish-speaking, Italian, Irish, hippie, addict, and criminal groups have been drawn from in different areas.

Various words and terms may be provincial and out of vogue. Some terms are very provincial in use and may be similar to "in house" jokes where only a small, particular "in group" understand.

Too immediate use of these terms to the group that initiate them by an outsider will meet with poor opportunities for rapport formations. Suspicion of patronage and condescension will alienate the individual and the group. Understanding by the professional or paraprofessional working with the group is the aim of this effort. Euphemistic spelling has been used for many of the terms because of the scarcity of available material to research. Provincial fads and fancies may be inferred where terms have similar meanings.

AC-DC	Bisexual
Acid	Psychedelic drug (LSD)
*Afro (or Bush)	Hairstyle
A-head	The user of acid
Ambidexterous	Bisexual
At	Where the action is—or I am
Ax	Musical horn or instrument
Babe	A person, usually female
Bag	Current fad or fancy—nice, consuming interest, business, trade, specialty, aptitude, caught in situation
Behind that	Following that—as a result of

---

* This list was updated before press time; asterisks indicate author's additions.

Exhibit 23 (continued)

Big Daddy	Strong-smart, person to respect and follow
Bitch-bitty	Girl, woman, complaint, easy make, nice
Blade	Knife, razor, sharp instrument
Blow	To play instrument, oral fornication, get away
Blow your mind or top	Overwhelming revelation, temper tantrum, out of your mind with drugs, squeal
*Boat	Car
Boo Hoo	Psychedelic or hippie priest or potentate, church
Boot	Kick, chase away, get rid of (*also, derogatory term for Negro)
Boots	Negro shoes
*Bootsie	Negro
Boss	Excellent, stylish, good
Box	Hi-fi set, phonograph, female sex organ, situation similar to "bag," guitar
Bread	Money, dust (*also, car)
Breaks me up	Upsetting, makes me laugh, affect positively
Broad	Girl or woman
Bug	Disturb, bother, annoy, intercourse
Bug out	Leave
Bull	Lesbian, sexually potent male
Bull-dagger	Lesbian
Burn	Shoot, cook, purchase of bad drugs, smoke pot
Busted	Out of money, get arrested, found out by significant persons
Butch	Lesbian with male attributes, recruiter for Lesbians, predator
Buy	Purchase drugs or pot
Cabbage	Money
Carrying	Have money or gun
Cat	Person
Catnip	Marijuana diluted with other ingredients, bogus marijuana
Change (carrying)	Money

Exhibit 23 (continued)

Changes	In emotion or feeling, as when using drugs, pot, and so on
Cherry	Virgin
Chick	Girl
Chippie	Girl on make, one who experiments with drugs
Chop	Food—used with up or down motion means to eat
*Clean	Well dressed, stylish
Clock	Wristwatch
Coins	Money
Coke	Cocaine or derivatives
Come	Sperm, orgasm, semen, ejaculate
Come down	Act in a certain way
Comes on	To act like or be similar to
Connection	To be in the know with someone in power or to make a buy from (as pot or drugs)
Contact	Same as connection
Contact high	To become "high" by close proximity to pot smokers
Cool	User of drugs, in or well informed
Cool it	Be quiet, tranquil; don't get excited
Coon	Negro
*Coon cage	Cadillac
Cop	To purchase or steal drugs
Cop out	Walk or run out on friends, fail to live up to responsibility, to purchase or steal a joint, not admirable thing to do
Crash	To break in, collapse from exhaustion while under the influence of drugs
Crib	House, residence, apartment house of prostitution
Cut a side	Make a record
Cut out	To leave, go away
Daddy-O	In or with the group
Dago	Of Italian extraction
Dapt	Stylish
Diddy bop	Gang member of hostile or aggressive group

Exhibit 23 (continued)

Dig	Understand, listen, pay attention, doing, being with and doing the action, such as doing or taking drugs
Dough	Money
Down	Depressed, low emotions
Drop out	Withdraw—from society, school, family; apex of psychedelic experience
Dust	Money
Fade	To go quietly
Fag	Queer—not accepted by group
Fall out	Same as drop out
Fed, Narc, Narco	Federal narcotics agent, undesirable
Flick	Movie
Flight	Take trip as under influence of drugs
Flip	Metaphor for mental cartwheel, withdrawal induced by pot or narcotics; response to music or other
Flower	Hippie instrument of self-defense
Fox	Girl, smart, crafty
Freak, Freak out	Bad drug experience, lose reality through drug use
Funny	Lesbian or homosexual
Fuzz	Police
Gang busting	Fighting groups or individuals
Gash	Easy girl to have intercourse with
Gay	Queer
Gestapo, Gestaps	Police
Get it	Understand, get with it emotionally
Git box	Guitar, banjo, mandolin
Go	Continue present activity, pep it up
Go conservative	No hostile or aggressive actions
Going social	Same as above
Goof	Act incorrectly, make mistake, act stupid
Goof off	Don't do job or follow responsibility
Goof on	Laugh at—make fun of—to mislead
Grab you	Positive reaction—affect
Grapes	Wino
Grass	Marijuana
Gray boy	Caucasian
Green	Paper money, dice gaming table

Exhibit 23 (continued)

Groove—as in the	Doing right, concentrate and enjoy immensely
Groovy	Pleasurable
Gripe	Complaint
Guide	One who gives guidance and support during psychedelic experience
Guru	Same as above, rabbi, spiritual leader, teacher
H	Heroin
Half	Homosexual
Hangup	Problem
Head	Drug addict; refers to emotional state of mind, as: "that's his head"
Headshop	Drugstore
Hick	Rural people, Puerto Rican youth, reference to immigrant parents
High	Elevated euphoric state induced by drugs or liquor
Hip	Nice, agreeable, favorable
Hitched	Marry, become partners
Holding	Have money
*Honky	White
Horn	Metal musical instrument
Horse	Heroin
Hurting	Broke, in trouble
Hustling	Prostituting, be aggressive, pimping, enterprising
Hype	Laugh at, put on, make fun of
I mean	Punctuation—I wish to say
Ice cream habit	On-off user of drugs
Ike	Hick, rural person, stupid
In	Involved, accepted, love-in, be in
Jack	Money
Jack up	Rob, steal, hold up
Jake	O.K.
Jam	To have intercourse, play musical instrument feverishly
Jap	Dishonorable
Jerk	Stupid person
Jim	Person—usually male
Jock	Stupid person, penis

Exhibit 23 (continued)

John	Bathroom, prostitute's customer
Joint	Penis, marijuana cigarette, place where liquor is served
Juice	Liquor, content for intravenous drug injection, money for bribe or payoff
Jump	Dance, fight, girl easy to have intercourse with
Junk	Drugs
Kicks	Ways of enjoyment, feeling of pleasure or success
Kiddies	People of lower status than speaker
Kike	Jewish person, or one who is stingy with money
Keyster	Buttocks
Later	Good-bye, farewell
Lay	Girl of easy virtue
Lay-up	Relaxing or place to rest or hide
Leg	Girl
Lid	Headwear, hat
Light up	Light marijuana cigarette
Like	Verbal punctuation used at end of sentences in place of comma or period
Liz or Lizzy	Lesbian
Loot	Money
M	Morphine
Machine	Automobile
Make it	To go away, to have intercourse, to be succesful
Man	Boss, top man, used as punctuation or greeting
Mandala	Indian design
Mantra	Indian chant
Marine Tiger	One Puerto Rican speaking of others who preserve old culture when brought to U.S.
Meat	Penis or a nonhomosexual who makes himself available for use by homosexuals
Member	Negro
Mickey Mouse	Caucasian
Mink	Girl friend

Exhibit 23 (continued)

Monkey	Unbreakable drug habit, member of other gang
Mother	Salesman of illegal drugs, leader of homos or lesbians
Mother F——	Derogatory term
Moulenjam	Negro
Mug	Stupid person, crude
Mugging	Steal from drunks, as in alleys
My people	Person with close ties, gang or neighborhood people, relatives
Nodding out	Drug or liquor stupor
Nowhere	Unacceptable person, strange
Nut	Mentally ill
Ofay	Caucasian person
Off-brand stud	Homosexual
Old Lady	Woman in man's life
Om	Universal mind or being
On it	Addicted to drugs
On the make	Prostituting, homosexual without partner
On the nod	Drug stupor
On your own	No one to help you, I'm leaving
*Oreo	Black on the outside, but with a white mind (and white attitudes and hang-ups)
Our leader	Top status in gang
Out of it	Disconnected state through use of drugs, removed, not in touch
Out of sight	Really good, superlative, amazing
Packing	Carrying pistol or knife
Pad	Residence, apartment, room
Paddy	Caucasian
Parakeet	Puerto Rican person
Peck	To eat
Pecker	Penis
Pick up	Purchase drugs or anything else, try to understand, appreciate
*Pig	Originally a term used to refer to white policemen, but now taking on a broader connotation to mean "white"
Pipe	Penis

Exhibit 23 (concluded)

Pluck	Wine or other liquor
Pop	To have intercourse, to be arrested, to have a drink of liquor
Pops	An older male person
Pot	Marijuana
Pound	Five dollars, money
Prez	Leader of hostile gang
Pudding	Good head, universal or cosmic mind
Pure silk	Homosexual
*Rags	Clothes
Rap	To talk, rapturous talk while under the influence of drugs (*usually berating whitey)
Rep	High status or reputation
*Rubber	Car
Rumble	Gang conflict
Sack	Jacket or coat, bed, place of rest
*Shaky	Not to be trusted; makes promises but never follows through
*Threads	Clothes

EXHIBIT 24. *Recommendations from the Shelly Report Prepared for The Urban Coalition*

In January 1969 The Urban Coalition published a report made possible by a grant from the Ford Foundation. The report, titled *Private Industry and the Disadvantaged Worker,* was prepared for the Coalition by E. F. Shelly and Company, Inc., and is based on questionnaire survey results from 224 major corporations (out of 273 approached) followed by personal interviews during field visits to 64 of those companies in 13 cities. Among the recommendations made in the Shelly report are the following:

1. The Government should continue the MA programs, reimbursing companies for extra training expenses in employing the hard core, rather than adopting alternative approaches, such as tax incentives. (The MA programs were found to be remarkably free of red tape.) In order to partially overcome corporate reluctance growing out of economic conditions, companies should be encouraged to approach training and upgrading programs as a research and development effort to meet long-term needs, rather than as a short-term profit-and-loss matter.

Exhibit 24 (concluded)

2. The Government should guarantee employment to all, perhaps as the employer of last resort, so an economic downturn will not erase minority employment gains.

3. The National Alliance of Businessmen should concentrate less on number of people hired, more on guiding the development of program structures to deal with management training difficulties. The consortium training approach is favored where there are many firms using similar job skills. Top corporate officials must be kept vitally involved in NAB, local coalitions, and other volunteer groups.

4. To keep top management involved, companies should appoint a high-level official with overall program responsibility, plus a staffer to deal with daily problems.

5. Efforts should be intensified to secure greater participation by suburban-based companies, either by establishing ghetto feeder plants or by providing more effective transportation to outlying areas. Central city companies are carrying most of the load now.

6. Remedial education programs should be linked specifically to the trainee's job opportunities and upgrading.

7. While companies cannot be expected to get too deeply involved in social services, they should develop a working knowledge of available community resources in this area.

8. To fill critical skill shortages and cushion the effects of automation, companies should do more upgrading of the low skilled for higher-level jobs.

9. Labor unions should be involved in program planning and implementation, at least when hard-core training programs can affect collective bargaining agreements or when a significant upbeat in minority hiring can arouse membership.

10. Given the current climate of racial hostility among low-income whites, and the inclination toward racial separatism among blacks, effective means of combating these problems on a short-range basis within an industrial environment have not been devised. What can be recommended, however, is corporate awareness that such problems can arise. Companies can prepare for these eventualities by developing soundly conceived program structures with built-in advancement opportunities, and by establishing channels of communication with white and black worker leadership.

7. A View from the Ghetto—
Some Personal Notes

THERE ARE SOME geographic ironies in our cities. From the steel-and-glass canyons of mid-Manhattan to the overcrowded and rat-infested slums of Harlem. From the tree-lined streets of suburbia to the garbage-strewn pavement of any ghetto. It is from the ghetto that the hard core come. It is from this environment that the occupants view affluent America. The view causes the viewers a great deal of pain as they observe but cannot have, dream but cannot expect to ever participate. The national program to bring the hard core into the economic stream is an attempt to make this dream of participation come true.

One of the purposes of this research study was to learn how all of this flurry of activity to employ the hard core is being perceived in the ghetto. Has the message really reached the hard core? Do they believe it? Certainly, the white business community has spared no effort to communicate its concern, again and again, in practically every business newspaper and magazine.

I conducted interviews in ghettos across America. I would spend the day talking to company executives, supervisors, and trainees and the evenings talking to people in the ghettos near these plants. The one common element in the ghetto interviews was anger, anger at continuing discrimination, anger at the high cost each felt he had to pay because of this. The few people who spoke with favor of the new drive for decent jobs for everyone were older people, usually recent migrants from the South. Among the young there is still a widespread and growing anger. The younger, the angrier.

In this chapter I will list excerpts from these interviews. I did not tape-record these interviews with residents of the ghettos, but rather tried to write down their words, as much as possible in their exact language, as soon as I had a convenient opportunity. Their words tell us much about the job ahead. One of the trainees in a hard-core program in a midwestern city told me this:

> It's a game, "professor," it's a big fat stinking game. Whitey gives up nothing, you dig? He's scared —— and comes running with a few crumbs. Sure they gave me a job, but it's at the bottom of the ladder. You're black. You know how much chance I got to get promoted or to make real money. All this crap about equal opportunity and jobs for all! It's the riots! Everybody knows that! Soon as it quiets down all the blacks will be back in the streets looking for those janitor jobs. It can't last, man. It can't last. The minute you begin to believe and trust the Man, the pig will kick you in the ass. So get what you can now, grab it now because it ain't going to last. It's the same old story with a new wrapper. We're still the last hired and the first fired. Hard-core unemployed is just crap. That report calling them racist was right. All this noise they are making has nothing to do with wanting to give you a chance. It is all aimed at stopping the riots. The minute black people stop raising hell, back we go to being janitors.

In a southern city, in a training session I observed that used the role-playing method to attempt to change attitudes among the hard core, one of the trainees came over during the break to talk to me about the session, a little bit embarrassed. He said:

> You know, this is a lot of ——. They think we're all afraid to talk to white people, to ask questions, or to speak up for the things we feel we are entitled to. That might have been the way it was before, but not today. This stuff we are doing is a waste of time. We want to learn a trade so that we can work. We go along with this stuff because they want it this way and it's their money. They may need to feel like they are doing something for us. And they got us acting like clowns.

In an eastern city a trainee I talked with had more encouraging things to say:

> I was a loser. I was twenty-four years old, a high school dropout, the usual jail record for taking someone else's car for a joy ride. I did my time, came out, got married, began the usual scramble

for a job. The questions were always the same: "Do you have a high school diploma?" "Have you any experience?" Or else the job was only part time and not enough pay to keep one person alive. My wife was working at the time and this is how we made it. Then she got pregnant and had to stop. The one or two jobs that I did land didn't last long because the shop didn't get enough work. This program is fine. I am learning to run printing presses and can earn much more money than I ever thought was possible. I didn't have to take any tests or show a high school diploma. The only question that they asked was if I wanted to learn a trade. They even run classes in school subjects and I am working on my high school diploma. Some of the fellows gripe about the program, but I guess they would gripe about anything. As far as I am concerned it's fine, one of the best things that could have happened to me. I was a loser and this program has made the difference with me.

The publicity received by a California company was nationwide and attracted attention across the country. The unwanted publicity also worked a hardship on the workforce. When I joined the great throng of visitors, one of the workers spoke to me privately and with great feeling:

We have been gaped at, photographed, and interviewed by almost every major firm in the country. It's to the point now that we ignore them. All this because we were the scene of a major riot. And now we are on display. We just want jobs and we would like to be left alone. The questions can be so ridiculous at times as if we are supposed to be unable to perform any kind of task. It got to be a game with some of us, giving ridiculous answers and making up stories that were believable but usually untrue. You would think they would understand that this is embarrassing to us, acting as if we are on display, some kind of freak. I am telling you this because you are black and might understand what I mean. But I guess this is part of the price of working today.

In a midwestern city a trainee expressed much gratitude about the whole idea of a good industrial job:

I came to Detroit in nineteen and sixty-three from a farm in Mississippi, where I had worked as a sharecropper. The work there was hard and the money one could earn was not hardly enough to buy food and clothes. I got a sister who had moved to Detroit several years ago during the Korean war. She had come here with her husband. She kept on writing to me and telling me to come because jobs paid more money and I might be able to get one. I've been here five years and there have been times when I wish I was back in Mississippi. Most good jobs could be had only if you passed a test or had a job like it somewhere else. I spent most of my working time doing odd jobs or jobs like helper or janitor. When I heard that they was going to come into the neighborhood to look for workers and that they wasn't going to give a test I reported the first day. It was in October and the place was suppose' to be opened for hiring at 7:30 in the morning. I was there at 6:30 and already there was a crowd. It was raining, but that didn't seem to matter to the people. Word had spread and I was afraid that they would not have enough jobs to go around. I had to come back two days later because they couldn't handle all the people that showed up. All they asked me when they hired me was if I wanted to work. No tests. Didn't even ask if I had a record. The pay was good. We were even offered bus fare the first week. We had physical exams right at the center. They told us to report for work the first of the following week. I've been here since October; my job at the plant is hard work, but the pay is good. I now belong to the union and things are going fine. I don't know what will happen if they have to lay people off. I know that the rules say the old-timers get to stay and us newcomers will be let go, but I hope this don't happen. This is the first real job that I ever had and the first time I ever been able to make this kind of money.

Some of the skepticism about American business' being "for real" this time—fairly widespread in the Negro communities—was expressed by a hard-core worker who completed all his training in a western company:

Yeah, it's fine right now. We got the jobs and they give us some training and it's lots better than it was before. But soon they got to make it real by letting some of us get promoted and not just let us stay in these beginning jobs. Some of us can become supervisors because some of us must have the ability, you know, and the real test comes when they have the chance to promote someone to see if they do. If the rest of us know that someone can get promoted it makes working here a lot easier. I don't mean they should promote somebody for a showpiece 'cause something like that just backfires.

The crucial role of the foreman in the formation of attitudes among the hard core who become employed was emphasized by a hard-core worker in a midwestern city:

> The difference whether you make it or not depends on the foreman you get. My foreman happens to be OK. He goes out of his way to help me, like, he stays after others have gone, to go over things with me, and shows me how to do some things easier. He does this without making you feel like you're stupid or like he is doing you a special favor. He's really OK with me. No comments about hard core or anything like that. He just says he wants a good crew and his job is to make it that way. Other fellows in the plant tell me that their foremen are not like this, that they act as if they don't want them there, and do little to help them, and make smart remarks sometimes even in front of them. I can understand them wanting to find a new job or transfer from the ones that they have. Like I said, I am lucky that my foreman isn't like this and that he treats me like a human being.

Another hard-core worker in the same plant described his experience:

> He's a red-neck, a cracker if I ever saw one and he is going to do his best to make it rough. Though he doesn't say it to my face you hear him making remarks about "giving them everything," how others had to work for what they got, but now all you have to do is raise a little hell and they have to give you the world. He offers me no help and is constantly complaining about my work and my attitude. His actions are copied by most of the people that work in the crew and it is a hard place to work. Two fellows before me left, one got a transfer, and the other just up and quit. I would complain to his boss, but you get a reputation of being a squealer and then it means the whole crew is down on you. The people who brought us in here should check back to see how we are doing instead of just dumping us and then going away. I'm not complaining about the program. It's a way out for me and most untrained people, but the foreman can make it very tough

if he wants to and unless someone higher up does something to keep them straight then we may be working and earning some money, but it can be pretty tough.

Because the heaviest concentration of attention in the business press has been on black people and urban programs, certain groups among the hard-core unemployed are receiving less help than they feel they deserve. In one western city I talked with a Mexican-American who had been through a hard-core training program and was working at a job he considered beneath his capabilities.

He said that in some ways it is even harder for a Mexican-American than a black American. He was kept in the third grade for three years because he couldn't master the English lessons that were taught. At his home, and in the homes of many Americans of Mexican descent, very little English is spoken. Everything is Spanish. He did complete high school, however, spending the majority of his time playing football. He said:

The only job I could find was a job too bad for whites. Even the job I have now is not much of an improvement. I don't think I'll ever get a promotion. But this is better than the agriculture-type jobs that most Mexican-Americans have to do. I've been treated fine here, no conflicts with the people I work with, but the job isn't much and they know that I'm not going to block anybody from a better job, or get promoted before they do, so they can afford to be nice.

In another city a very angry black man, a hard-core trainee, told me the following:

The thing that amazed me the most when I first reported to this job was how easy it was to learn the machine that I had to operate. All along they been saying you needed experience or they'd make you take some kind of test and this kept you out of a job. But once they hired without any test or didn't ask for a high school diploma, and you get into the job, you are surprised that you can work the machine without any trouble. You get mad at first when you realize that you have been kept out of work and from making good money by some fake excuse. No wonder black people are mad and want to break up things and start riots. I know I was mad when I got here and was put to work after a very short time. If they could do it now they could have done it a long time ago. All this time we have been kept away from making a decent living because of some fake rules. Another thing that bothered me was the people I work with acting like someone was doing me a favor to let me work and that I should be thankful for the job. Some of them even act like they had to do more to get their jobs than I did. I guess they're really mad 'cause we found out that most of it was just fake.

Finally, I spoke with people in California who are involved in the education of American Indians and who are trying to help them toward permanent employment outside the reservation. The focus of this effort is on the young. They lack formal education and skills needed by industry.

When older Indians come into the cities seeking work, the hardship is even worse. They are not at all familiar with the culture of the cities. Lacking money and jobs, they usually seek aid from welfare. If they are encouraged to return to their reservation, they resent it. Some Government-assisted programs have been started on their reservation to help them develop specific job skills before they come into the cities, such as welding and electronic-parts assembly. But they are often distracted and troubled by the breakdown of respect among their young, and the pace of change generally. They have been called the hardest of the hard core.

Appendixes

A special note of appreciation is extended to the staff members of AMA who did the research necessary to prepare the material in these Appendixes: Helen Wisely, Research Assistant; Phyllis Lindemann, Literature Researcher; Paul London, Program Director—Trainee; and Donald Lilenfeld, Senior Management Information Counselor.

MANY COMPANIES that have developed programs to employ the hard-core unemployed have found that their vital interests demanded increasing attention to the problems that, taken together, constitute what has been described as the Urban Crisis. For these companies, and other companies now developing an interest in solving urban problems, an extensive literature search was undertaken to provide information on the breadth and variety of company programs that have been launched. It should be noted, however, that the business-Government-institutional attack on urban problems is fast moving, and there is mobility on many fronts. As a result, information presented here may not be current and complete by the time this research study is printed. The lists are intended to help a company develop a running start in its research to discover the state of the art in urban affairs problem solving.

Contents of the appendixes:

1. Key Programs of the Federal Government.
2. Examples of Companies Attacking Urban Problems in Ways Other than Job Training or Money Contributions.
3. Selected Reading.
4. A Partial List of Motion Pictures Dealing with the Nature of Prejudice, Hard-Core Problems, and Action Programs.

1. KEY PROGRAMS OF THE FEDERAL GOVERNMENT

AFFIRMATIVE ACTION PROGRAM. Program set up by the Equal Employment Opportunity Commission to provide funds, technical assistance and to help business achieve equal employment goals.

COMMUNITY ACTION PROGRAM (CAP). An Office of Economic Opportunity (OEO) program that sets up Community Action Boards on a local level to aid antipoverty programs.

CONCENTRATED EMPLOYMENT PROGRAM (CEP). Program of the Department of Labor to provide recruiting, training, counseling, and employment services and to coordinate other Federal programs in the area of manpower.

COOPERATIVE AREA MANPOWER PLANNING SYSTEM (CAMPS). Department of Labor Program set up to coordinate Federal programs with resources at regional, state, and local levels.

DEPARTMENT OF HEALTH, EDUCATION, AND WELFARE (HEW). Makes grants to local school districts to provide necessary skills training for underprivileged youths to prepare them for jobs.

DEPARTMENT OF HOUSING AND URBAN DEVELOPMENT (HUD). Makes grants in fields of urban transportation, housing, community facilities in urban renewal areas.

THE ECONOMIC DEVELOPMENT ADMINISTRATION (EDA). Under the Department of Commerce, provides loans for industrial development to specific economic areas.

HEAD START. Program to provide preschool aid to underprivileged children. OEO-sponsored.

JOB CORPS. Voluntary OEO program to provide basic education and job-skill training for youths 16 to 21.

JOB OPPORTUNITIES IN THE BUSINESS SECTOR (JOBS). Government program in cooperation with the National Alliance of Businessmen to reimburse employers of hard core for training costs.

MANPOWER DEVELOPMENT AND TRAINING. Department of Labor's program to provide occupational training for unemployed. Also provides on-the-job training as well as basic education.

MODEL CITIES PROGRAM. A Housing and Urban Development (HUD) program using hard core as labor to aid in the renewal of slum areas.

NATIONAL ALLIANCE OF BUSINESSMEN (NAB). Joint effort of Government and business to locate jobs for the hard core.

NEIGHBORHOOD YOUTH CORPS. OEO-sponsored program to provide basic education, training, and jobs for over 400,000 youths.

NEW CAREERS PROGRAM. Department of Labor's program for adult work training, educational counseling, and other assistance to enable trainees to hold permanent jobs.

OFFICE OF BUSINESS PARTICIPATION (OBP). Under Housing and Urban Development, helps business solve housing problems.

OFFICE OF ECONOMIC OPPORTUNITY (OEO). Part of the Labor Department, which operates a number of antipoverty programs.

OFFICE OF FEDERAL CONTRACT COMPLIANCE. Part of Department of Labor, set up to insure nondiscrimination among Government contractors or subcontractors.

OFFICE OF MANPOWER AUTOMATION AND TRAINING (OMAT). Division of Department of Labor responsible for carrying out programs of the Manpower Development and Training Act (MDTA).

OPERATION MAINSTREAM. Department of Labor program to establish work-training and employment projects for hard-core unemployed.

PROJECT TRANSITION. Established by the Defense Department to ease the return of servicemen to civilian life by providing counseling, education, skills training, and job placement.

SERVICE CORPS OF RETIRED EXECUTIVES (SCORE). Part of the Small Business Administration, set up to provide advice to small-business owners.

SMALL BUSINESS ADMINISTRATION (SBA). Helps train and finance small businesses. Introduced loan guarantees for Negro businesses to aid black enterprise.

SPECIAL IMPACT PROGRAM. Department of Labor's funding of projects for work training in poverty areas.

STATES URBAN ACTION CENTER (SUAC). Program established by Federal Government to assist state governors on urban problems.

TECHNICAL ASSISTANCE CONSULTING TEAM (TACT). OEO project working with institutions and using the resources of Volunteers in Service to America (VISTA).

UPWARD BOUND. OEO program to give precollege aid to ghetto youths.

URBAN INSTITUTE. Federal "think tank" for research on urban problems.

VOLUNTEERS IN SERVICE TO AMERICA (VISTA). Volunteer domestic peace corps working in poverty areas. OEO-sponsored.

VOLUNTEERS TO AMERICA. Volunteers from abroad to help solve community-development and poverty problems in the United States.

WORK INCENTIVE PLAN (WIN). HEW's program to provide training and supportive services to unemployed parents of dependent children.

2. EXAMPLES OF COMPANIES ATTACKING URBAN PROBLEMS IN WAYS OTHER THAN JOB TRAINING OR MONEY CONTRIBUTIONS

Locating Plants in Poverty Areas

A&E PLASTIK PAK COMPANY. Plastic container company; will build a new plant in depressed East Los Angeles and hire 335 from the area.

ADVANCED HUDSON MOUNTING & FINISHING COMPANY, INC. Advertising display firm relocating to Bedford-Stuyvesant.

AVCO CORPORATION. Handles about one-third of its printing needs in a converted cigar factory employing 150 newly trained workers, mostly Negroes and Puerto Ricans, in Boston's Roxbury section. Will expand into Dorchester slum. Training minority employees for management. AVCO organized a consortium of black contractors to build the new plant.

BROWN SHOE COMPANY, INC. Opening a new plant in St. Louis slum area, which will employ over 200 hard core.

CONTROL DATA CORPORATION. Leased building in Northside Minneapolis slum to produce computer components. Hiring local manpower—100 employees. Another plant in planning.

FAIRCHILD CAMERA & INSTRUMENT CORPORATION. Moved into a plant on the Navajo reservation at Shiprock, N.M. Fairchild makes transistors in the leased plant built with Navajo tribal funds.

GENERAL DYNAMICS CORPORATION. Started electronics-assembly plant in Fort Defiance, Ariz., and a shipping-crates plant in San Antonio; both plants employing Navajos.

GENERAL ELECTRIC COMPANY. Opened plant in Phoenix ghetto for processing metal scrap and is training hard core in its large lamp factory in the Newark, N.J., ghetto area.

INTERNATIONAL BUSINESS MACHINES CORPORATION. Leased an old warehouse in Bedford-Stuyvesant and is turning it into a computer cable factory, which will employ 300 residents.

NORTH AMERICAN ROCKWELL CORPORATION. Formed a subsidiary, Nartrans, which supplies metalworking, woodworking, keypunch, and other products and services to North American Rockwell. Its management is largely Negro, and its workforce is primarily hard core.

J. C. PENNEY COMPANY, INC. and F. W. WOOLWORTH COMPANY. Will open branches in St. Louis ghetto and Harlem respectively.

VOGUE INSTRUMENT CORPORATION. An electronics company building a new plant in Jamaica, Queens, N.Y., on a site acquired by New York City under a new "vest pocket" industrial renewal program.

WESTERN ELECTRIC COMPANY, INC. Designed its Newark and

Baltimore ghetto plants to train workers for regular plants rather than to become profit centers. Efficient workers will be transferred to other production facilities.

WESTINGHOUSE ELECTRIC CORPORATION. Will build new plant in Homewood-Brushton section of Pittsburgh.

Establishing Plants and Transferring Control to the Local Management or the Community

AEROJET-GENERAL CORPORATION. Started tent-making subsidiary, Watts Mfg. Co., in Watts. Supplying Defense Department contract, has black management and employees. Expanded into metalworking and wooden containers. Profits will be shared, in cash or stock, by Aerojet and the employees of Watts Mfg. Co.

EG & G, INC. A diversified avionics and instrument firm; has established a light-metal fabrication plant in Roxbury, with plans to sell 75 percent control of the plant over 20 years to black management, workers, and the community.

WARNER & SWASEY COMPANY. Established Hough Mfg. Co. to produce such products as shipping pallets, hospital equipment, and jobshop work and will buy many of its products. It will be black-managed and eventually black-owned. Hard core will be employed. Warner & Swasey will also lend expert personnel.

Helping Establish Operations to Be Operated and Owned by Minority Groups

CROWN ZELLERBACH CORPORATION. Helped start the San Francisco Container Corporation in Hunter's Point, Calif., with the aid of the Bay Area Management Council and the Bank of America.

FAIRCHILD HILLER CORPORATION. In a joint venture with District of Columbia's Model Inner City Community Organization (a Negro self-help group), formed Fairmicco, Inc. Backed by money from Fairchild, the group, and the U.S. Government. Will sell stock and become a community-owned organization. Makes loading pallets for the Government, wiring harnesses, and circuit boards.

GENERAL ELECTRIC COMPANY, MISSILES & SPACE DIVISION. Subcontracted $2.6 million of business to Progress Aerospace Enterprises Inc., a black-owned-and-administered company formed with the help of Rev. Leon Sullivan. It is situated in the North Philadelphia ghetto. Most of Progress Aerospace's managerial talent is provided by half a dozen black technical and administrative men hired from General Electric.

XEROX CORPORATION. With FIGHT, formed Fighton, an electrical-transformer and metal-stampings manufacturing company in Rochester, N.Y. It will be wholly black-owned and will employ about 100 people. Xerox will provide a full-time manufacturing expert and a financial analyst, other technical advice, and a guarantee to purchase $500,000 worth of products for each of the first two years.

Making Technical Assistance Available to
Minority-Owned Operations

CHASE MANHATTAN BANK. Has made block-by-block visits to 400 black-owned businesses in Harlem to find loan prospects and has directed more than two dozen officers and staff members to give advice and encouragement to developing Negro businesses.

RADIO CORP. OF AMERICA. Trained 100 hard core to repair toasters, vacuum cleaners, and larger appliances. Later offered substantial help to hard core in setting up their own repair shops in the ghetto.

RAYTHEON COMPANY. Provides six company specialists in physics, chemistry, mathematics, and astronomy to advise and assist teachers, counsel guidance personnel on employment openings and standards, and improve curricula in Boston's public schools.

SAFEWAY STORES, INC. Bought 800 bushels of potatoes for retail sale in its supermarkets from a cooperative made up of impoverished Negroes in Louisiana. With a six-man consulting team, it is helping the blacks of Hunters Point sustain a cooperative supermarket established by ghetto investors, who paid $5 a share.

SHEARSON, HAMMILL & COMPANY. Investment firm. Opening a branch in Harlem and establishing an independent foundation to provide investment capital, business guidance, and job opportunities in Harlem. The foundation will be financed with 7½ percent of the gross commissions of the branch.

SWIFT & COMPANY. Has helped six Negroes establish ice cream parlors in Chicago.

Making Financial Resources Available to Benefit
Minority Individuals or Enterprises

BANK OF AMERICA. Allocating up to $100 million in real estate loans to aid home-building efforts in minority neighborhoods of California.

FIRST PENNSYLVANIA BANKING & TRUST COMPANY. Established program of extending loans to black businesses in poor neighborhoods. Appointed a specific branch to implement the program. Some loans have SBA guarantees.

FORD FOUNDATION. Has established a Program Related Investment

Account, whereby the foundation will channel a small portion of its invested funds into high-risk operations that benefit ghetto economic development.

HANCOCK. Pledged to buy $100,000 worth of stock to launch Unity National Bank, a multiracial bank in Roxbury.

METROPOLITAN LIFE INSURANCE COMPANY and PRUDENTIAL INSURANCE COMPANY OF AMERICA. Led insurance companies in making $2 billion available for loans for ghetto housing.

OLIN MATHIESON CHEMICAL CORPORATION. Deposited large sums of money in six Negro-controlled banks to be available for loan to Negro businesses.

PHILLIPS PETROLEUM COMPANY. Plans to invest $20 million to help 250 Negroes, Eskimos, Mexican-Americans, Puerto Ricans, and Orientals open and manage service stations.

SOUTHERN CALIFORNIA EDISON COMPANY. Deposits its income tax withholding funds of about $50,000 a month in the Bank of Finance, a predominantly Negro bank in Los Angeles.

Adopting High Schools and Giving Educational Assistance

ÆTNA LIFE & CASUALTY. Adopted Weaver High School in Hartford. Assisting the school newspaper, providing space for examinations, teaching special courses. Also offering driver's training to minority youths at company expense as an aid to job placement.

CHRYSLER CORPORATION. Has adopted Northwestern High School in Detroit.

COMMONWEALTH EDISON COMPANY. In Chicago, about 100 company employees have worked as volunteer tutors with ghetto children.

CONTINENTAL CAN COMPANY, INC. Has ten centers to provide basic educational skills to employees.

E. I. DU PONT DE NEMOURS & COMPANY. Established "Upward Bound" program to encourage school dropouts to stay in school.

EASTMAN KODAK COMPANY, ROCHESTER, N.Y. Designed and developed self-help programs with the aid of the Board for Fundamental Education.

HONEYWELL, INC. and GENERAL MILLS, INC. Joined to assist the Minneapolis school system to develop and run programs designed to motivate inner city students to continue their education.

INTERNATIONAL BUSINESS MACHINES CORP. Aided by the Bank of America Foundation, helped greater Los Angeles Urban League open computer job training center.

MICHIGAN BELL TELEPHONE COMPANY. Has adopted Northern

High School, 98 percent black, in Detroit. Makes available manpower, technical and management skills, and training facilities. Michigan Bell managers give night and Saturday courses designed to help students find employment when they graduate.

WISCONSIN TELEPHONE COMPANY. Runs special summer program to keep potential dropouts in school by providing counseling and training.

Requiring Nondiscriminatory Policies from Suppliers

FORD MOTOR COMPANY. Called major suppliers and told them it expected equal rights in all their organizations.

NEIMAN-MARCUS. Dallas department store; told its 2,000 suppliers that it will favor those who act to train and employ members of minority groups.

Examples of Consortiums or Cooperative Ventures

BALTIMORE CONSORTIUMS. A 46-member Baltimore consortium, with the Chamber of Commerce of Metropolitan Baltimore, will hire and train 418 hard-core unemployed under the NAB-JOBS program. An 11-member Baltimore employer consortium will train and hire 80 hard core as meat cutters in cooperation with the NAB program.

CELANESE CORPORATION. Heads a consortium of companies in conjunction with Columbia University's Urban Action and Experimentation Program to build low-cost housing.

KOPPERS COMPANY. Along with a 20-member consortium, formed Allegheny Housing Rehabilitation Corp. (AHRCO) to rehabilitate housing in Pittsburgh area.

LOCKHEED MISSILES & SPACE CO. Managing a consortium of 41 companies in the San Francisco area in training the hard-core unemployed.

MANPOWER, INC. (MILWAUKEE). Heading a national 11-company consortium in training the hard core.

NEW DETROIT COMMITTEE. Businessmen and civic leaders organized to rebuild Detroit after riots.

NEW JERSEY. Eight pharmaceutical companies formed The Pharmaceutical Technical Training Project for training hard core as lab technicians for employment in the drug industry.

NORTH CITY CORPORATION. Fifty business representatives of North Philadelphia organized to improve job opportunities, educational facilities, and housing for hard core.

PITTSBURGH. The Greater Pittsburgh Chamber of Commerce and a

28-member consortium will train and hire 106 hard-core jobless under the JOBS program.

Other Projects

BOSCOV'S. Department store in Reading, Pa., sponsored in its stores a Negro Heritage Festival, which featured Negro leaders in education, science, art, theater, fashion, sports, entertainment, and government.

CLAIROL. Sponsors with the New York City Urban Action Task Force a leadership program to build self-esteem in teen-age girls in Harlem. Kenwood Reter furniture store supplies space for the program, which includes discussions of fashions.

JOB SYSTEM. Computerized system developed by Information Science, Inc. to match hard core with entry-level jobs or training opportunities on a nationwide basis. Developed with the aid of the National Association of Manufacturers.

MIND, INC. A subsidiary of Corn Products to provide prejob training in basic subjects geared for the hard core. Program used successfully by several companies.

SMITH KLINE & FRENCH. Wrote part-time responsibility in the Spring Garden neighborhoods into the job descriptions of two community-relations executives. Established an Information Services Center, providing information and advice in health care, food, clothing, and so on to local residents.

WHIRLPOOL CORPORATION. Doing research studies on day-care centers.

3. SELECTED READING

Publications by the American Management Association

Ahern, Eileen, "Equal Employment Opportunity: The Civil Rights Law and Voluntary Programs," *Personnel,* July-August 1965.

Ash, Philip, "Selection Techniques and the Law: I. Discrimination in Hiring and Placement," *Personnel,* November-December 1967.

Bird, Caroline, "More Room at the Top: Company Experience in Employing Negroes in Professional and Management Jobs," *Management Review,* March 1963.

Callender, Eugene S., "The Ghetto Subculture," *Personnel,* May-June 1968.

Dewhurst, John D., "Employing the Unemployables," *Supervisory Management,* June 1968.

Gassler, Lee S., "How Companies Are Helping the Undereducated Worker," *Personnel,* July-August 1967.

Gourlay, Jack G., *The Negro Salaried Worker,* Research Study No. 70, 1965.

Haakenson, Robert, "The Urban Crisis: What One Company Is Doing," *Management Review,* July 1968.

Heltzer, Harry, "Poverty Is Our Business," *Personnel,* March-April 1968.

James, J. Hahan, "Guidelines for Initiating Fair Employment Practices," *Personnel,* May-June 1963.

Jensen, Jerry J., "Developing Fair Employment Programs: II. A Program for the Smaller Company," *Personnel,* July-August 1966.

Kirkwood, John H., "To Test or Not to Test?" *Personnel,* November-December 1967.

Lockwood, Howard C., "Developing Fair Employment Programs: I. Guidelines for Selection," *Personnel,* July-August 1966.

McDonald, Charles H., "Supervising the 'Unemployable,' " *Supervisory Management,* February 1969.

Mayfield, Harold, "Equal Employment Opportunity: Should Hiring Standards Be Relaxed?" *Personnel,* September-October 1964.

"Merit for Hire: How On-the-Job Integration Has Worked Out in Leading Companies," *Supervisory Management,* May 1968.

Metzler, John H., "Testing Under Labor Contracts and Law," *Personnel,* July-August 1966.

Mobilizing for Urban Action, based on AMA's Special Conference, June 3–5, 1968.

The Negro Worker, Special Research Report No. 1, 1942.

Palmer, Edward H., "Finding—And Keeping—Minority Group Managers," *Personnel,* January-February 1969.

Riessman, Frank, "New Careers: A Workable Approach to Hard-Core Unemployment," *Personnel,* September-October 1968.

Turrentine, James L., "A Corporate Program for Urban Action," *Personnel,* July-August 1969.

General References

Adams, Charles F., "The Urban Crisis," *Vital Speeches of the Day,* July 1, 1968.

Albrook, Robert C., "Business Wrestles with Its Social Conscience," *Fortune,* August 1968.

Beardwood, Roger, "The Southern Roots of Urban Crisis," *Fortune,* August 1968.

"Bringing New Jobs into the Ghettos," *Business Week,* December 2, 1967.

Burck, Gilbert, "A New Business for Business: Reclaiming Human Resources," *Fortune,* January 1968.

"Business and the Urban Crisis," *Business Week,* February 3, 1968.

"Business and the Urban Crisis," (Special Issue), *Fortune,* January 1968.

"Business Bridge to Racial Progress," *Nation's Business,* October 1967.

"Business Rebuilds the Slums," *Nation's Business,* June 1967.

Callender, Eugene S., "The Urban Crisis," *Vital Speeches of the Day,* July 1, 1968.

Champion, George, "Creative Competition," *Harvard Business Review,* May-June 1967.

Chasen, Robert E., "The Urban Crisis," *Vital Speeches of the Day,* July 1, 1968.

"Crisis in the Cities: Does Business Hold the Key?" *Dun's Review,* November 1967.

Davis, Walter G., "The Urban Crisis," *Vital Speeches of the Day,* July 1, 1968.

"Dealing the Negro In," *Business Week,* May 4, 1968.

Gilmer, Ben S., "Business Involvement in Urban Problems," *Business Horizons,* June 1968.

Ginzberg, Eli (ed.), *Manpower Agenda for America,* McGraw-Hill, New York, 1968.

Glasgow, Robert W., "The Urban Crisis," *Psychology Today,* August 1968.

Gullander, W. P., "Preacher of Pragmatist Role of Industry in the Urban Crisis," *National Association of Manufacturers,* Urban Affairs Division, New York, July 15, 1968.

Haynes, Ulric, Jr., "Equal Job Opportunity, The Credibility Gap," *Harvard Business Review,* May-June 1968.

Henderson, Hazel, "Should Business Tackle Society's Problems?" *Harvard Business Review,* July-August 1968.

Hodge, Claire C., "The Negro Job Situation: Has It Improved?" *Monthly Labor Review,* January 1969.

"Investing in Economic Progress and Social Order," *Conference Board Record,* National Industrial Conference Board (NICB), February 1968.

Javits, Jacob K., "The Urban Crisis," *Vital Speeches of the Day,* July 1, 1968.

Jensen, Arthur R., "How Much Can We Boost IQ and Scholastic Achievement?" *Harvard Educational Review,* Winter 1969.

Kalb, W. J., "How Businessmen and the Ghettos Can Get Together," *Iron Age,* May 30, 1968.

Killingsworth, Charles C., *Jobs and Income for Negroes,* Institute of Labor and Industrial Relations, The University of Michigan, Ann Arbor, Mich., 1968.

Kleinschrod, Walter A., "White-Collar Jobs and the Hard-Core Unemployed," *Administrative Management,* April 1968.

MacNamee, Holly, "Learning the Hard Facts of Hard-Core Unemployment," *The Conference Board Record* (NICB), August 1968.

Marcus, Stanley, "Who Is Responsible: A Businessman Looks at Civil Rights," *Business Horizons,* June 1968.

Marshall, Charles, "Civil Rights: What Role for Business, I. The Next Move Is Ours," *Saturday Review,* January 13, 1968.

The Negro Handbook, Johnson Publishing Company, Inc., Chicago, 1966.

"The Negro in America," *Newsweek,* November 20, 1967.

"Point and Counterpoint on Employing the Jobless," *Business Management,* August 1968.

"Pushing Harder for Ghetto Jobs," *Business Week,* January 20, 1968.

"Putting Blacks in the Black," *Nation's Business,* December 1968.

"Racism Challenges Union Leadership," *Steel,* March 17, 1969.

"The Response of Business to the Problem City," *The Conference Board Record* (NICB), February 1968.

Ross, Arthur M., and Herbert Hill (eds.), *Employment, Race and Poverty,* Harcourt, Brace & World, New York, 1967.

Ryscavage, Paul M., and Hazel M. Willacy, "Employment of the Nation's Urban Poor," *Monthly Labor Review,* August 1968.

Social and Economic Conditions of Negroes in the United States, Bureau of Labor Statistics, No. 332, Washington, D.C., 1967.

Star, Jack, "A National Disgrace: What Unions Do to Blacks," *Look,* November 12, 1968.

Sturdivant, Frederick D., "The Limits of Black Capitalism," *Harvard Business Review,* January-February 1969.

"The Unions State Their Case," *Fortune,* February 1968.

Wellman, David, "The Wrong Way to Find Jobs for Negroes," *Trans-Action,* April 1968.

"What Can Business Do for the Negro?" *Nation's Business,* October 1967.

What Can You Do About the Hard-Core Unemployed? Research Institute of America, Inc., 1968.

"White-Collar Jobs and the Hard-Core Unemployed," *Administrative Management,* April 1968.

"White Collars for the Hard Core," *Modern Office Procedures,* September 1968.

Legal Aspects

Bullock, Paul, *Equal Opportunity in Employment,* Institute of Industrial Relations, University of California, Los Angeles, Calif., 1966.

The Civil Rights Act of 1964, The Bureau of National Affairs, Inc., Washington, D.C., 1964.

"Employment of Negroes by Government Contractors," *Monthly Labor Review,* July 1964.

"Equal Employment Opportunity Act of 1966," (as passed by the House of Representatives on April 27, 1966), *Fair Employment Practices No. 31,* The Bureau of National Affairs, Inc., Washington, D.C., April 28, 1966.

Equal Employment Opportunity in Federal Government on Federal Contracts, Executive Order No. 10925, The President's Committee on Equal Employment Opportunity, Washington, D.C., 1961.

Fair Employment Practices Under Federal Law, Commerce Clearing House, Inc., Chicago, Ill., 1966.

Flower, Barbara J., "Law, Order, and the Businessman," *The Conference Board Record* (NICB), December 1968.

"Hiring and Promotion Policies Under Federal Legislation," *Monthly Labor Review,* February 1967.

Leventhal, Sharon, "Job Discrimination Is Illegal: A Guide to Legal Action," *Public Affairs Pamphlet No. 400,* The Twentieth Century Fund, Inc., New York, 1967.

Miller, Richard B., "Civil Rights and Your Employment Practices," *Personnel Journal,* Swarthmore, Pa., 1965.

Viot, Van H., "The Corporation and Title VII," *The Conference Board Record* (NICB), April 1966.

"What Business Can Do for the Negro," *Nation's Business,* October 1967.

Adaptation of Company Employment Procedures

Company Experience with Negro Employment, *Studies in Personnel Policy* No. 201 (NICB), 1966.

"Employing the Unemployables: What Companies Are Finding," *U.S. News & World Report,* August 12, 1968.

Finding Jobs for Negroes: A Kit of Ideas for Management Manpower and Automation, U.S. Department of Labor, Washington, D.C., 1968.

Francis, David R., "U.S. Business Makes Workers from Hard-Core Jobless," *The Christian Science Monitor,* July 12, 1968.

A Guide to Negro Media: Magazines, Newspapers, Radio, and College, prepared by Deutsch & Shea, Inc., New York, N.Y., 1968.

"Hiring of Minority Folk by Dailies, Magazines Come Next, Booth Says," *Advertising Age,* January 27, 1969.

"How to Turn Dropouts into Steady Workers," *Business Week,* August 31, 1968.

Reynolds, William H., *Experience of Los Angeles Employers with Minor-*

ity Group Employees, Report to Management No. 16, Graduate School of Business Administration, University of Southern California, Los Angeles, Calif., March 1967.

Samuels, Gertrude, "Help Wanted: The Hard-Core Unemployed," *The New York Times Magazine,* January 28, 1968.

"Training the Unemployables: What One Company Learned," *U.S. News & World Report,* July 1, 1968.

"Want More Negro Applicants? Recruit at Prime Sources," *Employee Relations Bulletin,* November 11, 1964.

"Why Does Quaker Back Program in Ghetto? Because 'It Needs to Be Done,' " *Advertising Age,* February 17, 1969.

The "Affirmative Action" Program

"Answers to Urban Crisis: A Survey of Mayors on Ills and Remedies; Are Model Cities the Business of Business? Managing a War on Poverty," *Nation's Business,* February 1969.

"A Business Attack on Poverty—Training the 'Unretrainable,' " *U.S. News & World Report,* March 18, 1968.

Effectively Employing the Hard Core: An Aid to Companies Joining the Growing Efforts of the Industry to Help Resolve Basic Social Problems, National Association of Manufacturers, Urban Affairs Division, New York, 1968.

"Getting a Ghetto Back in Shape," *Business Week,* March 23, 1968.

"An Industry's Cure for Slums," *U.S. News & World Report,* September 2, 1968.

Janger, Allen R., "Employing the High-School Dropout," *The Conference Board Record* (NICB), August 1968. "New Start—For the Hard Core," *The Conference Board Record* (NICB), February 1969.

McFarlane, Alexander N., "Leaping the Ghetto Gap," *The Conference Board Record* (NICB), March 1969.

Manpower Report of the President, U.S. Department of Labor, Washington, D.C., 1968.

"Negro-Owned and -Managed Plant Fills Big Ghetto Need—Jobs," *Modern Manufacturing,* September 1968.

"A Positive Action Program for Equal Job Opportunity," *Employee Relations Bulletin,* March 3, 1965.

Purcell, Theodore V., "Break Down Your Employment Barriers," *Harvard Business Review,* July-August 1968.

"Removal of Artificial Barriers Opens Hiring Door to Hard-Core," *Employee Relations Bulletin,* August 14, 1968.

"The Response of Business to the Problem City," *The Conference Board Record* (NICB), February 1968.

"Teach Hard Core Interpersonal Skills," *Employee Relations Bulletin,* September 4, 1968.

Webster, Staten W. (ed.), *The Disadvantaged Learner,* Chandler Publishing Co., San Francisco, Calif., 1966.

Wellman, David, "A Job for Negroes That Flopped," *Business Management,* June 1968.

Testing

"Are Psychological Tests Fair? Experts Cast Light on Complex Problem," *Employee Relations Bulletin,* June 2, 1965.

Barrett, Richard S., "Gray Areas in Black and White Testing," *Harvard Business Review,* January-February 1968.

Employment Testing: Guide Signs, Not Stop Signs, U.S. Commission on Civil Rights, Washington, D.C., August 1968.

Guidelines on Employment Testing Procedures, Equal Employment Opportunity Commission, Washington, D.C., 1966.

Guion, Robert M., "Employment Tests and Discriminatory Hiring," *Industrial Relations News,* Industrial Relations Counselors, Inc., New York, February 1966.

"How to Get a Better Understanding of That Hard-Core Applicant," *Industrial Relations News,* Industrial Relations Counselors, Inc., New York, September 1968.

Kirkpatrick, James J., *et al., Testing and Fair Employment,* New York University Press, New York, 1968.

Lockwood, Howard C., "Testing Minority Applicants for Employment," *Personnel Journal,* July-August 1965.

"New Tools for Getting the Unemployed into Jobs," *Manpower,* January 1969.

Samuels, G., "Help Wanted: The Hard-Core Unemployed; Detroit Experiment by the Ford Motor Company," *The New York Times Magazine,* January 28, 1968.

Hiring

"Employing Ghetto Workers: Nine Lessons of Experience," *Management Thinking,* July 1968.

Habbe, Stephen, "Hiring the Hard-Core Unemployed," *The Conference Board Record* (NICB), June 1968.

"The Hard-Core Enters the Work Force," *Occupational Hazards,* May 1968.

"How to Prepare for the Hard-Core's Entry," *Occupational Hazards,* May 1968.

"How to Succeed in Hard-Core Hiring," *Business Week,* August 24, 1968.

"Redesigned Application Form Takes Ghetto Life into Account," *Employee Relations Bulletin,* November 20, 1968.

"The Unfinished Business of Negro Jobs," *Business Week,* June 12, 1965.

"Will 'John Garth' Make It?" *American Machinist,* June 3, 1968.

Special Guidance and Training for Supervisors

"Awareness Training," *Industrial Relations News,* Industrial Relations Counselors, Inc., New York, September 28, 1968.

Clark, Kenneth B., "No Gimmicks, Please, Whitey," *Training in Business and Industry,* November 1968.

Employing the Negro in American Industry, Industrial Relations Counselors, Inc., New York, 1959.

"Equal Employment Seminars Help Shape Management Attitudes," *Employee Relations Bulletin,* December 21, 1966.

"Industry Looks at the Negro Supervisor," *Steel,* October 23, 1967.

Kurzman, Stephen, *Private Enterprise Participation in the Antipoverty Programs,* U.S. Senate, Committee on Labor and Public Welfare, Subcommittee on Employment, Manpower and Poverty, Washington, D.C., 1967.

"Managers Must Avoid Discrimination," *Iron Age,* July 18, 1968.

Perkins, John A., "Managers and the Solution of Urban Problems," *The Conference Board Record* (NICB), February 1969.

"A Quick Way to Upgrade Your Blue-Collar Workers," *Business Management,* August 1967.

Development and Training Programs for Employed Minority Personnel

Catalog of Federal Assistance Programs. (A description of the Federal Government's Domestic Programs to Assist the American People in Furthering Their Social and Economic Progress.) Office of Economic Opportunity, Executive Office of the President, Washington, D.C., June 1, 1967.

Chansky, Norman M., *Untapped Goods,* Charles C. Thomas, Springfield, Ill., 1966.

Drob, Judah, and Vernon Sheblak, "Training the Hard-Core Unemployed," *Manpower,* January 1969.

"Employing the Unemployables; What Companies Are Finding," *U.S. News & World Report,* August 12, 1968.

Gourlay, Jack G., "The Negro in Business and Industry," in *The Business World: Introduction to Business Readings,* by R. Joseph Monsen and Borje O. Saxberg, Houghton-Mifflin Company, Boston, Mass., 1967.

Hodgson, James D., and Marshall H. Brenner, "Successful Experience: Training Hard-Core Unemployed," *Harvard Business Review*, September-October 1968.

Hoos, Ida R., *Retraining the Work Force; An Analysis of Current Experience*, University of California Press, Berkeley, Calif., 1967.

"Intensive Training for 'Unemployables' Pays Off," *Steel*, November 18, 1968.

"Jobless Training Begins with ABC's" *The New York Times*, June 16, 1968.

"The Los Angeles Project: What One City Is Doing for Hard-Core Jobless," *U.S. News & World Report*, February 12, 1968.

McKamy, Kent, "Putting the Jobless to Work: Toughest Part Still Ahead," *Business Management*, June 1968.

Marshall, Ray F., and Vernon M. Briggs, Jr., *The Negro and Apprenticeship*, The Johns Hopkins Press, Baltimore, Md., 1967.

Methods of Job Development for the Hard-Core Unemployed, Proceedings of Conference, October 1–2, 1968, Georgia Institute of Technology, Atlanta, Ga., January 1969.

Negroes in Apprenticeship, Manpower/Automation Research, No. 6, U.S. Department of Labor, Manpower Administration, Washington, D.C., August 1967.

Northrup, R., *The Negro in the Automobile Industry*, University of Pennsylvania, Philadelphia, Pa., 1968.

Report of the National Advisory Commission on Civil Disorder, The New York Times Company, New York, 1968. (See Chapter 7—"Unemployment, Family Structure, and Social Disorder"; Chapter 17—"Recommendations for National Action.")

Shaeffer, Ruth G., "Big Brother to the Disadvantaged," *The Conference Board Record* (NICB), March 1969.

Strauss, George, "The Negro and Apprenticeship: A Review Article," *Journal of Human Resources*, Summer 1968.

"Teaching People to Hold Jobs: The Philadelphia Plan," *U.S. News & World Report*, January 1, 1968.

Training the Hard-Core, a 12-volume manual being prepared under the sponsorship of the Urban Coalition and the National Alliance of Businessmen, Urban Research Corporation, Chicago, Ill., 1968.

"Training the 'Hard-Core'—A Top Banker Tells His Story," *U.S. News & World Report*, August 12, 1968.

"Training the 'Hard-Core' for Private Jobs," *U.S. News & World Report*, February 12, 1968.

Urban and Government Programs

"As I See It" (interview with James Gavin), *Forbes,* October 1, 1968.

"Bankrolling the Slum Clearance Jobs: Insurance Companies," *Business Week,* October 14, 1967.

Birch, David L., *The Businessman and the City,* Harvard University Press, Boston, Mass., 1967.

"Blacks Wrap Up Slice of Action at Food Chains," *Business Week,* April 26, 1969.

"Boston Companies to Train Jobless," *The New York Times,* July 14, 1968.

Business Amid Urban Crisis, Studies in Public Affairs, No. 3 (NICB), 1968.

"Business and Race: Big Companies Venture Their Talent and Money in Civil Rights Effort," *The Wall Street Journal,* June 14, 1968.

"Business and the Urban Crisis," *Business Week,* February 3, 1968.

"Business Now Backs Cleveland," *Business Week,* September 21, 1968.

Cervantes, Alfonso J., "To Prevent a Chain of Super-Watts," *Harvard Business Review,* September-October 1967.

Cohen, Vincent, "59 Groomed for Building Craft," *Washington Post,* September 3, 1968.

"Companies Answer the Call for Ghetto Jobs," *Business Week,* June 15, 1968.

Cowles, Arthur W., "Businessmen and Negro Leaders Weigh Their Current Concern," *The Conference Board Record* (NICB), July 1968.

Garrity, John T., "Red Ink for Ghetto Industries?" *Harvard Business Review,* May-June 1968.

McKersie, Robert B., "Vitalize Black Enterprise," *Harvard Business Review,* September-October 1968.

Manpower Report of the President, Department of Labor, Washington, D.C., April 1968.

Mayors Evaluate Business Action in Urban Problems, Supplement to Studies in Public Affairs, No. 3, National Industrial Conference Board, 1968.

National Conference on Corporate Urban Programs: An Investment in Economic Progress and Social Order, Public Affairs Conference, No. 6, National Industrial Conference Board, New York, 1968.

Patten, Thomas H., Jr., *Literacy Training and Job Placement of Hard-Core Unemployed Negroes in Detroit,* School of Labor and Industrial Relations, Michigan State University, East Lansing, Mich., 1968.

Progress Report of the New Detroit Committee, New Detroit Committee, Metropolitan Fund, Inc., Detroit, Mich., 1968.

Putting the Hard-Core Unemployed into Jobs, U.S. Department of Justice, Community Relations Service, Washington, D.C., 1968.

The Quiet Revolution, Office of Economic Opportunity, Washington, D.C., 1965.

Report of the Governor's Committee on Employment of Minority Groups in the News Media, Office of Governor Nelson A. Rockefeller, State Capitol, Albany, N.Y., April 1969.

Robinson, Marion O., *Humanizing the City,* Public Affairs Pamphlet No. 417, The Public Affairs Committee, Inc., New York, 1968.

Sanders, Charles L., "Industry Gives New Hope to the Negro," *Ebony,* June 1968.

"Training the 'Hard Core' for Private Jobs," *U.S. News & World Report,* February 12, 1968.

Unemployment and Retraining: An Annotated Bibliography of Research, U.S. Office of Manpower, Automation, and Training, Washington, D.C., 1965.

"Washington: A Look Ahead; Can Do-Gooding Be Profitable?" *Nation's Business,* February 1968.

Watson, John H., III, and Grace J. Finley, "Business Support of Education for the Disadvantaged," *The Conference Board Record* (NICB), May 1968.

Weeks, Christopher, *Job Corps,* Little, Brown and Co., Boston, Mass., 1967.

4. A PARTIAL LIST OF MOTION PICTURES DEALING WITH THE NATURE OF PREJUDICE, HARD-CORE PROBLEMS, AND ACTION PROGRAMS

THE BRIDGE

20 min, 16mm, b&w; produced by and available from The National Association of Manufacturers, Film Bureau, 277 Park Avenue, New York, N.Y.

Bridging the gap between the high school dropout and the world of work.

DAY IN THE NIGHT OF JONATHAN MOLE

29 min, 16mm, b&w; available from Contemporary and McGraw-Hill Films, 330 West 42nd Street, New York, N.Y.

Discussion of the causes and consequences of racial prejudice and its effect on the chances for fair employment.

EMPLOYING THE DISADVANTAGED

45 min, 16mm, color; available from B.N.A. Films, 5615 Fishers Lane, Rockville, Md.

Documentary on the approaches and techniques in five different industry programs for hiring and training the disadvantaged.

MAKING IT

    27 min, 16mm, color; produced by American Can Co., New York, N.Y. Available on loan from Modern Talking Picture Service, 1212 Avenue of Americas, New York, N.Y.

Twelve black men who have "made it" tell how they feel about their jobs and discuss qualities that they feel helped them to succeed.

MANAGEMENT, MOTIVATION AND THE NEW MINORITY WORKER

    43 min, 16mm, b&w & color; available from Roundtable Films, Inc., 321 South Beverly Drive, Beverly Hills, Calif.

Panel-discussion format, including a role-playing situation between a hard-core trainee and a first-line supervisor.

THERE MUST BE A CATCH TO IT

    12 min, 16mm, b&w; sponsored by The United States Employment Service. Available through the information offices of local state employment services.

Illustrated approach to problems encountered in interviewing minority applicants.

WILLIE CATCHES ON

    24 min, 16mm, b&w; available from the Audio-Visual Library, National Conference of Christians and Jews, 43 West 57th Street, New York, N.Y. (or regional chapter offices).

How we learn to be prejudiced.

SOURCES OF CATALOGS AND INFORMATION ABOUT ADDITIONAL MOTION PICTURES AVAILABLE

Audio-Visual Library, National Conference of Christians and Jews, 43 West 57th Street, New York, N.Y.

Contemporary Films/McGraw-Hill, 330 West 42nd Street, New York, N.Y. *Films of Social Comment* (Catalog).

Olympic Film Service, 161 West 22nd Street, New York, N.Y. *Training the Disadvantaged;* subscription, $30 a yr. (Monthly Film Profiles).

Sterling Movies, Inc., 43 West 61st Street, New York, N.Y.